George Worley

The Catholic Revival of the Nineteenth Century

George Worley

The Catholic Revival of the Nineteenth Century

ISBN/EAN: 9783744724609

Printed in Europe, USA, Canada, Australia, Japan

Cover: Foto ©Lupo / pixelio.de

More available books at **www.hansebooks.com**

THE CATHOLIC REVIVAL

OF

THE NINETEENTH CENTURY.

A BRIEF POPULAR ACCOUNT OF ITS ORIGIN, HISTORY, LITERATURE, AND GENERAL RESULTS.

Six Lectures
BY
GEORGE WORLEY.

WITH AN INTRODUCTION
BY
THE DEAN OF ST. PAUL'S.

> 'Diseases desperate grown
> By desperate appliance are relieved,
> Or not at all.'
> *Hamlet.*

LONDON:
ELLIOT STOCK, 62, PATERNOSTER ROW, E.C.
1894.

To the

REV. C. P. GREENE,

Rector of Clapham,

UNDER WHOSE AUSPICES THESE LECTURES WERE GIVEN,

THE VOLUME IS INSCRIBED,

WITH THE AUTHOR'S KIND REGARDS.

CONTENTS.

	PAGE
INTRODUCTION	ix
PREFACE	xiii

LECTURE I.
A PRELIMINARY VIEW OF THE CHURCH OF ENGLAND — 1

LECTURE II.
PRECURSORS OF THE REVIVAL — 26

LECTURE III.
THE OXFORD MOVEMENT: ITS LEADERS AND SUPPORTERS — 57

LECTURE IV.
THE OXFORD MOVEMENT—*continued* — 76

LECTURE V.
THE LITERATURE OF THE CATHOLIC REVIVAL — 94

LECTURE VI.
SOME FRUITS OF THE CATHOLIC REVIVAL — 122

INTRODUCTION

AT the request of the author of the following lectures I have gladly consented to write a short introduction to them. I have been greatly struck by the thoughtful attention with which my friend of many years' standing has followed the fortunes of the religious movement about which he writes, amid the constant occupations of a commercial life. He has evidently not only read the principal books upon the Oxford Movement, but he has pondered over them, and, after mastering them, has endeavoured to utilize the information so acquired for the benefit of those possessed of less knowledge and leisure than himself. The lectures were delivered substantially as they now appear to large gatherings of Sunday-school teachers. Mr. Worley became acquainted with them through his own active labours as a Sunday-school teacher, and in his endeavours to promote lectures and other instrumentalities by which those self-denying Church workers might be assisted to fulfil more efficiently the important duty which they had undertaken. The special value of these lectures appears to me to lie in their viewing the Oxford Movement from a different standpoint to that of any of the works on the subject which have hitherto appeared. In the pamphlets upon the earlier history of the Oxford tracts which were written by Mr. Perceval and Mr. Palmer, in the 'Apologia' of Dr. Newman, in the history of the Oxford Movement by Dr. Church, and in the autobiography of Mr. Isaac Williams, we have a faithful record of the progress of events by men who took an active part in the occurrences which they narrate. In the 'Lives of Twelve Good Men,' by the late Dean Burgon, and in Dr. Liddon's 'Life of Dr. Pusey' we have reliable detailed accounts of what occurred from those who lived in daily intercourse with the persons whose biographies they write, and who were themselves deeply interested in, and thoroughly cognizant of, the events which they describe; whilst in portions of Dean Stanley's 'Life of Dr. Arnold' and in his own biography by Mr. Prothero we have an account of the Oxford Movement as it appeared to opponents. But in the writers thus named friends and foes were alike members of the same University, and therefore naturally regarded events from an academic point of view, and under the influence of impressions aroused by personally taking part in the many contests, literary and otherwise, which brought their respective opinions into collision. There are no such personal relations with the people named in Mr. Worley's view of the movement.

He probably never spoke to any of the writers with whose opinions he sympathized. He watched the progress of events from the outside, deeply interested in what was happening, feeling that his own religious opinions were being formed on principles which these writers advocated, but nevertheless able to take that unimpassioned view of events which City life naturally encourages. We have, therefore, in what he has written a fair and faithful statement concerning the great religious movement of our time from a lay point of view by an earnest commercial man, who took a delight in reading whatever was written on either side by influential persons whose words were likely to carry weight. And in the views of one such man we probably have a key to the opinions of many others similarly circumstanced. In this consists the special value of the following pages, which, it will be seen, cover so much of the ground before the date of the Tract-writers as is likely to interest those persons of a later generation who really care for the subject, but who have not shared in the anxieties of the time of which they speak, and who do not possess the opportunity or leisure necessary to enable them to master the details of what happened during the years with which they are concerned. To those so circumstanced who wish to gain a correct idea of the more important incidents connected with the Oxford movement, I can confidently recommend the following lectures. Whilst not committing myself to perfect agreement with all the statements advanced, I can confidently say that, so far as I have been able to study them, they may be relied upon for the substantial accuracy and fairness with which they are placed before the reader.

ROBERT GREGORY.

THE DEANERY, ST. PAUL'S.
September, 1894.

PREFACE.

THE following Lectures were delivered at Clapham during last Lent to a number of teachers and others interested in the subject. They are reproduced for the sake of those who heard them and wished to see them in a permanent form, as well as for any others who may think them useful in teaching or sufficiently interesting for their own perusal.

It is hardly necessary to say that, although the account here given of the Catholic Revival is contained in that small compass which the nature of the case required, it represents a good deal of reading, as may be gathered from the references and quotations which occur in these pages.

Rightly to understand the Revival, it has been necessary to know something about the history and literature, ecclesiastical and general, which preceded it, as well as the books brought forth by the Tractarians, their critics and opponents, during and after the Oxford Movement. 'The publications of these men,' the Rev. T. Mozley observes, 'in whatever rank or degree attached to the cause, whether movers, original writers, translators, whether organized, or taking their own lines, amount to an enormous mass of literature sufficient to tax students in time to come.'

I had got through much of this reading in a random sort of way long before I had any thoughts of applying it to a special purpose, so that when the opportunity occurred I had merely to systematize and arrange information previously obtained, and supplement it with such special reading as I could get through on the spur of the moment. In addition to reading, I have drawn on my memory for certain facts, opinions, and practices which have come under my observation from time to time, and which, as far as I am aware, are found in no books. In both cases, however, I have taken pains to verify what I have said, so that, on the whole, the account here given is as close to the truth as I could make it. Still, in sending a book of this or any other kind to the publisher, one cannot help some misgivings such as those expressed by M. Renan with regard to his letters: 'Quand je relis ce que j'ai écrit, je m'aperçois que le morceau est très faible, que j'y ai mis une foule de choses dont je ne suis pas sûr. Par désespoir, je ferme la lettre, avec le sentiment de mettre à la poste quelque chose de pitoyable.' However, my good friend, the Dean of St. Paul's, has been kind enough to take me under his wing in the shape of an Introduction, of which, as an unknown writer, I gratefully avail myself, as well as of his valuable suggestions towards improving the text.

GEORGE WORLEY.

Michaelmas, 1894.

THE CATHOLIC REVIVAL OF THE NINETEENTH CENTURY.

LECTURE I.

A PRELIMINARY VIEW OF THE CHURCH OF ENGLAND.

THE removal of abuses in the Church was the main object of the early Reformers and their adherents. They were animated by a destructive and innovating temper, which was at once a necessary consequence of the abuses they sought to remove and the cause of their success in removing them. I am not going to criticise either the men or their motives now. Suffice it to say that our Church owes them a great debt of gratitude for shaking her free from the fetters cast around her in the Middle Ages, for liberating her from the dominion of Rome, for asserting the rights of individual reason and conscience, for breaking down a great deal of superstition, and for securing us a liberty in belief and practice which we might never have enjoyed but for them. It must be obvious, however, to every impartial student of Church history that their policy was *de*structive rather than *con*structive. Necessarily so; for when men are smarting under a tyrannous system they naturally seek to destroy it before substituting another whose existence is incompatible with it, and, in fact, impossible while the tyranny endures.

In this respect the Reformation is something like the French Revolution. The excesses in both cases were largely the result of previous misgovernment; the excesses were to a great extent inevitable; and the movements are rather to be judged by their permanent results than by their contemporaneous evils. Shakespeare says:

> 'The evil that men do lives after them,
> The good is oft interred with their bones.'

In great political and ecclesiastical movements the position is often reversed. Evils frequently die with the movements that give them birth; posterity enjoys their benefits. And in England the disastrous consequences of the Reformation were less obvious and less lasting than on the Continent. Our insular position, and the natural conservatism of English character, though not preventing the Reformation from taking effect here, exercised upon it a restraining influence which was not felt to the same extent in Germany. Here two forces were simultaneously at work; there was a desire for reform, but there was also that reverence for ancient landmarks which has always been displayed during the great crises of English history. It is to this reforming, though conservative, spirit, this co-existence and combination of apparently opposing, though not really inconsistent, forces, that we owe the peculiar character of our Book of Common Prayer. It obviously represents and provides for two different schools of thought; one in such parts as the Thirty-Nine Articles (or the popular interpretation thereof), and other productions of the Renaissance period; the other in those stately forms and creeds which have been retained from earlier times.

During the great reign of Elizabeth the rival forces of innovation and conservatism were frequently in collision, and it became manifest to the leading spirits on either side that there was a line beyond which they could not follow each other. It was during this reign that the Puritan separation from the Church occurred, and the chief divines on the Church side became alive to the necessity for supplementing the work of the earlier and more destructive reformers by some definite scheme of theology, without which the Church system, which was not based on a mere *argumentum ad hominem*, but required a special education rightly to understand and appreciate, would fail to commend itself to the general public. It was at this crisis that the 'judicious Hooker' arose, and wrote his books on the Ecclesiastical Polity of the English Church, which have lost none of their savour by the lapse of three centuries (the first four books were published in 1594), and are still appealed to as an authority on the doctrines and ritual of the Church of England.

Hooker was followed by a series of writers representing what has appropriately been called the Anglo-Catholic school of theology—the school, that is, which, while recognising the peculiarly Anglican nature of our Church, is yet alive to the evils of separating her entirely from universal Christendom, and especially from the doctrines and practices (where these can be clearly ascertained) of primitive Christianity. Amongst the great divines of the Stuart period were Dr. Lancelot Andrewes, Bishop of Winchester; Dr. Christopher Sutton; Archbishop Laud; Dr. Hall, successively Bishop of Exeter and Norwich; Dr. Hammond, Chaplain to King Charles I.; Bishop Jeremy Taylor; Dr. Leighton, eventually Archbishop of Glasgow; Dr. Brevint, Dean of Lincoln; Simon Patrick, Bishop of Ely; Dr. Addison, Dean of Lichfield; Dr. Ken, Bishop of Winchester; Dr. Sparrow (like Hall), Bishop of Exeter and Norwich; Dr. Beveridge, Bishop of St. Asaph; and, somewhat later, the saintly Bishop Wilson, of Sodor and Man.

Lord Macaulay, in his drastic style, says that Laud never wrote anything above the capacity of an old woman. This remark, by the way, should be placed side by side with Carlyle's hasty expression that Keble had no more brains than an ordinary rabbit. I cannot suppose that either of these critics seriously meant what he said, or that either had read much of the man he was speaking about. Anyhow, it is now generally admitted that the chain of theologians I have mentioned (Laud included) have left in their works a precious treasure to the Church of England—a body of theology which will hold its own with the writings of any other school or period.

These writers were succeeded, and their doctrines carried on, by the Nonjurors, who suffered deprivation under William and Mary, from a conscientious objection to transfer their oath of allegiance from James II. to the new rulers. In them the Church of England lost some of her brightest ornaments, from whose loss she suffered, I may say, till the date of the religious revival we are going to study.

The Caroline divines and Nonjurors were replaced by theologians of a different type, but it would be wrong to suppose that their opinions were entirely extinguished within the Church. Here and there were isolated Churchmen who still held their unfashionable doctrines, and based their teaching and preaching on their writings. The latter had special weight with clergymen of a literary turn; for it is an indisputable fact that the opposite school, though not destitute of great names, had done nothing, as a whole, which could rank as permanent ecclesiastical literature.

The incomparable sermons of Jeremy Taylor, Barrow, and South furnished nutriment to their successors, who, though not perhaps able to produce such stuff of their own, were quite able to appreciate what these men had left behind them, and were quietly in sympathy with their doctrines. Still, on the whole, the bulk of English clergymen, from the accession of William and Mary down to the opening of the present century, necessarily held opinions which were certainly not Catholic, nor, indeed, spiritual, until, under the influence of Whitefield and Wesley at the end of the last century, the school called 'Evangelical' arose.*

For this state of things there were other than religious causes. The second branch of the Stuart family were of somewhat different churchmanship from their predecessors, and most members of the House of Brunswick have been out of sympathy with the Church of England. I do not mean that they have been hostile to it; but they had been led to identify it with the political party which was scarcely friendly, certainly not *actively* friendly, to themselves, and the political bias was assisted by the theology which they

---

* In the Rev. T. Mozley's 'Reminiscences of Oriel,' there is a suggestive, though perhaps somewhat exaggerated, contrast between the High Church and the Evangelical clergyman. He says:

'It was the High Churchman who was pastor. The two things went together naturally, for the High Churchman assumed all in his parish to be his flock, all to be Christians—all on the road to heaven, though requiring much help, guidance, and stimulus. Of course he had to work quietly. There was no one to report or publish his talk. His best things were said to one at a time. A hard day's work would not be known even in the next parish. Talking daily with poor country people, he became more and more like them—for we all grow like those we are most with. His sympathies preyed on his purse as well as his strength, and after a long spell of this work even an able man would become fit for it and for nothing more.

'The part of the Evangelical preacher was the very opposite of all this. The great mass of the people committed to his care he assumed to be utterly bad or hopelessly good—that is, hopelessly trusting to good works; or perhaps waiting for the day and hour when the divine call was to reach them. . . . He could thus reserve his attention for a few, and would naturally consult his own tastes and preferences in the selection. Relieved thus from the dull reiteration of house to house work, and from close parochial duty generally, he became mobilized. He preached and heard preaching; he spoke from platforms and heard speeches; he came across missionaries, philanthropists, and the flying staff of societies. He saw something of the higher, richer, and more educated classes. . . . These clergymen were known, while the others were unknown. Evangelical preachers were announced and paraded . . . they sought the most capacious and best situated churches, and long before the Oxford Movement rich partisans were fast buying up the most important pulpits for them.'

brought with them from Germany. Of the Church of England as a branch of the Catholic Church they had little or no conception. Various other forces were at work to diminish the influence of the Anglo-Catholics. Amongst them, I think we must reckon the wars in which England was engaged with France during the latter part of the last, and the early part of this, century. The absurd ideas of the frog-eating Frenchman were extended to the Church to which he was supposed to belong, and whatever comparisons were set up between one and the other people and their respective religions were naturally unfavourable to the foreigner. Having been blessed with such victories as Trafalgar and Waterloo—although there were many who, like Napoleon, held that the Almighty was always on the ide of the strongest armies—there was a notion floating in .he public mind on this side of the Channel that we were specially favoured by Providence as the custodians of the Gospel; and that particular form or portion of it which happened to be popular at the time was, not unnaturally, regarded as the right religion. And, further, England was so elated at her victories, and held such prestige throughout Europe, that by a very easy mental process the credit of her transactions was assumed as the reward of her national high qualities. And besides, so much interest centred in the secular considerations consequent on a victorious campaign, that religious considerations were subordinated or excluded. With her success England became extremely worldly. All this was, of course, intensified by the active co-operation with Germany, where Protestantism prevailed.

The Georgian era has been called the *siesta* of the English Church. It was a period of indifference and apathy as far as religion is concerned; but now and again the darkness was relieved by an electric flash, as it were, from the skies. In 1726 William Law (a Nonjuror) published his ' Serious Call to a Devout and Holy Life,' a book to which Dr. Johnson tells us he owes his first religious impressions.

Somewhat later we have the rising of that great star on the horizon, John Wesley. It is worth noticing that *his* first serious thoughts were also attributed to Law's work, together with Bishop Taylor's immortal 'Holy Living.' Christianity in this country owes very much to the revival effected by the Wesleys, Whitefield, and other like-minded preachers. Their appeals, however, were rather directed to the emotions than to the intellect. They attempted to convert the individual soul—a very necessary work, but obviously elementary. The building up of the individual in the faith, as well as the holding together of numbers of people, requires this elementary work to be supplemented by a system, by regular teaching and regular practices, such as the Church provides, but which were very much in abeyance in those days, and whose want the revivalists themselves did not live long enough to realize. We thus see that three forces were in operation to the detriment of the Church of England, viz. :

(1) The Erastianism of the dominant party among the clergy ;

(2) The engrossing nature of political and national subjects, which excluded ecclesiastical matters from the public mind, or at least obscured them ; and

(3) The predominance of emotional over dogmatic and intellectual teaching.

I do not deny that each of these suggests interests which have a legitimate place among the objects of human thought and attention; but as far as the Church of England is concerned, their united weight was too heavy for her healthy life and movement. Men lost the idea of the Church as an independent organized body, free to exercise its functions apart from the State, and as a Divinely-appointed society for the custody of the truth, and responsible for the religious education of the country.

The legislation of the early part of this century, as far as it affected the Church, was only the practical application of the public idea concerning it, and was of course damaging, or at least disturbing, *e.g.*, the removal of Nonconformist and Romanist disabilities. These, as we know, have since been followed, as a necessary consequence, by the removal of Jewish and atheist disabilities; but that the leaders of the Church were not quite destitute of their old independence was strikingly illustrated at the time of the Reform Bill, when the bishops exercised their legislative functions by voting against it. The result was a threat from its exasperated promoters, couched in the historical words directing them to 'set their houses in order.' And in 1834 Lord Ripon actually introduced a Bill (though it was rejected by 125 votes against 28) to suspend the legislative and judicial functions of the Lords spiritual.

We can easily understand the growth of a belief among Churchmen, who still retained any of the older notions about the Church's independence, that the then rulers of the country were bent on its destruction. The suppression of ten Irish bishoprics, in defiance of Church opinion, showed how ready the Government was to take liberties with the time-honoured connection between the Church and realm, which was now used as a lever to invade the rights and to tamper with the constitution of the former. The resisting power of the Church was rendered almost nugatory by the suspension of her convocations. Under circumstances which we need not go into now, these fell into abeyance in 1717, and were indefinitely prorogued till the middle of the present century.*

As practically interwoven with the State, the Church, at best, possesses little independent action. Its articles, liturgy, organization as to benefices, etc., are all affected by civil statutes, while its discipline falls within the scope of the ecclesiastical courts, a class of tribunals apart from the ministering clergy. The Church, even under the most favourable circumstances, has a very limited jurisdiction,

---

* The Provinces of Canterbury and York were respectively allowed a semble in 1852 and 18 6.

and in the absence of convocation her weakness was of course intensified. She had no means of consultation or expressing her opinion as a body, and the prevailing sentiment on religious matters had nothing to correct it except the isolated utterances of individual Churchmen, amongst whom there was no sort of combination or mutual understanding that could be at all effective. It was felt very generally in the secular world that it would be safer for the public to be under the authority of Parliament than subject to a body of ecclesiastics, who were likely to run into excesses, and to put forth claims adverse to the ruling political and religious opinions of the day, and there was consequently no disposition in the State to give back to the Church any of the powers which she was thought to have forfeited.*

This brings us very roughly to the condition of the Church in 1833, when John Keble preached his celebrated sermon on 'National Apostasy,' which has always been regarded as sounding the keynote of the revival. The title seems a strong one, but it is scarcely too much for the condition of things to which it refers.

I have hitherto spoken of general principles rather than details; but perhaps I had better go into the latter a little, as illustrating the state of the Church better than any mere generalities on the subject. When I was a little boy two pictures used to figure in the shop-windows. These bore the names of 'Brimstone' and 'Treacle.' The first represented the enthusiastic and eloquent young Mr. Spurgeon, full of subjects suggested by the well-known yellow mineral, and the place where bad people were supposed to go. 'Treacle' represented the typical Evangelical preacher of the day, with his hair carefully oiled and combed, with black kid gloves upon his hands, which rested delicately upon the enormous cushion then adorning the pulpit. His

* See Dr. Littledale's article on 'Convocation' in 'Chambers's Encyclopædia.'

dress was the collegiate black gown, over which was thrown a black stole of enormous width, and from his collar depended two little white oblong flaps, technically known as 'the Commandments,' from a fancied resemblance to the two tables of the law. The preachers represented by these types practically divided the religious world between them. With the celebrated Nonconformist we have, of course, nothing to do except as illustrating a reaction against the insipid platitudes of the Evangelical pulpit. The latter was still under the influence of such divines as James Hervey, author of 'Theron and Aspasio' and 'Meditations among the Tombs.'* He died in 1758, but his works enjoyed an amazing popularity till well into this century, and his style was much admired till Coleridge exposed its absurdities, and helped to diminish the writer's influence. Another rather later writer of the same school was the celebrated Legh Richmond, author of 'The Young Cottager' and 'The Dairyman's Daughter,' who died in 1827.

Both these writers are now quite neglected. If anyone will take the trouble to read a few pages of their works he will notice the following characteristics: There is a great deal of what would now be regarded as false sentiment, more moralizing than would now be used, very little historical information, except such as is purely scriptural, still less of anything that can be called dogmatic teaching, and there is absolutely nothing requiring an intellectual

* Hervey's 'Meditations' suggests epitaphs and other monumental inscriptions which throw an interesting light on the religious taste of the eighteenth, and early nineteenth, century. There is a curious correspondence between the architectural and literary styles. The visitor to Westminster Abbey cannot fail to be struck by the monstrous design of many of the tombs and the enormous length and flattering language of many of the inscriptions, which contrast so unfavourably with the simple commemorations of earlier times, say, of the Norman abbots in the Cloisters. The same want of taste is shown in tombstones in every churchyard. There is rather a conspicuous instance at Norwood Cemetery, in the tomb of Sir John Gilbart, who lies under several tons of marble completely covered with an essay on Banking.

effort to understand. Great stress is laid on faith, and, although good works are not taught for their own sake, a great deal of importance is given to moral goodness. The effect of the whole is soothing rather than stimulating; they are not controversial, except now and then, when they point out the errors of Rome and the advantages of Protestantism. The conversion of the individual is a *sine quâ non*, and so is the duty of prayer; but no stress is laid on Church principles or the sacramental system. I have quoted these two writers because it was on such models that the evangelical preacher based his style. Their characteristic qualities, whether beauties or blemishes, were those of the school. With every disposition to acknowledge their good influence, we must admit that they were deficient in precisely those points which were most wanted in the lax Churchmanship of their day. And no one will suppose that the average preacher was up to the standard of his best models. In the first quarter of this century the sermon had sunk very generally to the level of a mild and easy sedative, which quieted men's consciences with a sense of duty performed in having listened to it, without requiring more mental effort than was sufficient to produce a pleasurable sensation in the listener. The enunciation of duties generally unobserved, and feelings which could not be realized, or which were of no practical value, fell Sunday after Sunday with a soothing monotony on the ears of those who listened or fell asleep. There was no practical influence on the people; the sermons were not clever enough for the intellectual, and not stirring enough for the uneducated. The searching philosophy and poetical illustration of the Stuart divines had long passed away; the intense earnestness and vigour of the Methodists had followed, and the pulpit had lost its power.

And yet the sermon still occupied a very important place in the Sunday arrangements. The fact is evidenced by the form of pulpit (now obsolete) called a *three-decker*. It consisted of three stages: the first for the clerk, the second for the reader of the prayers and lessons, the third and highest for the preacher. This huge erection, which was sufficiently high to command the galleries, used to stand at the east end of the nave right in front of the altar, the view of which it completely obscured. The altar itself was a diminutive table as a rule, with the alms-dish standing up on edge at the back in the place now usually occupied by a cross, supported on each side by a bulky cushion, on which the officiating clergy were wont to rest their elbows or bury their heads while kneeling at their respective ends.

The pulpit and the altar were typical of the relative positions of preaching and the Sacraments in the popular judgment of the day. We all know that it is possible to make too much of any single department in the Church system. In the Middle Ages too much importance was attached to sacerdotalism and the sacramental side of Church life. Some of us have perhaps been in danger of repeating the error. Certainly we are in danger of neglecting the educational value of preaching. But in the first quarter of this century the pulpit was glorified, and the 'balance of power' was destroyed.

In those days a wretched system of *free seats* was in full vigour. At the back of the galleries, or in some other obscure corner, these frightful free seats used to stand, with their name written on them in bold characters, as if to mark the humble condition of their occupants. Sometimes, indeed, they were placed in a more conspicuous position— *e.g.*, down the middle of the nave. This arrangement was better for seeing and hearing; but the advantages were very doubtful, counterbalanced as they were by exposure to a cross-fire from the well-dressed congregation on either side.

But wherever the free seats were, they were always uncomfortable—instruments of torture, in which the victim could neither sit nor kneel easily; in which, as a rule, he could see little and hear less. In many respects they remind one of the cheap seats at a theatre, except that there was less of a scramble to get into them, for they were seldom overcrowded. The Church of England was felt to be the Church of the respectable, well-dressed, and well-to-do classes. The poor were made to feel very emphatically that even in Church they were in the presence of their superiors; and, as if to mark as distinctly as possible the distance between those in the free seats and those who rented their sittings, the pews were raised to a height which completely concealed their occupants from the vulgar eye, except while standing, when their heads were just visible above the ledge. The doors, moreover, were often provided with locks and keys. Of course, it was right that the pews should be guarded safely, for they were paid for, and were often fitted up at the holders' expense with carpeting, cushions, and hassocks, besides small cupboards for the service books, sometimes even with sofas, tables, and fireplaces. Dean Swift's verses may occur to some of us as a humorous description of the pews of his time:

> 'A bedstead of the antique mode,
> Compact of timber many a load;
> Such as our grandsires wont to use,
> Was metamorphosed into pews;
> Which still their ancient nature keep
> By lodging those disposed to sleep.'

Cases have been known—though possibly before the time we are speaking of—where the tedium of a long service, or the appetite engendered by it, has been relieved by the entrance of a livery servant, between prayers and sermon, with sherry and light refreshments.*

---

* It appears that pews had undergone some reduction since the time of Bishop Corbet of Norwich, as his language concerning them would scarcely be applicable in the nineteenth century. He died in 1635. His remarks are as follows:

'Stately pews are now become tabernacles, with rings and curtains to them. There wants nothing but beds to hear the Word of God on. We have casements, locks, keys, and cushions—I had almost said

When a gentleman entered his seat it used to be the correct thing for him to go through the process known as 'smelling his hat,' which consisted of holding that article of costume gracefully in the right hand, and looking into it for a minute or so (if such an expression may be used when the eyes were closed) while saying his preparatory prayer. I do not know whether this practice was dependent on the hat being quite new, but I never saw a shabby hat used for the purpose. Anyhow, it was not the custom to *kneel* for prayer, either before or during service. In the latter case an indolent compromise was adopted, the seat being retained, while the head was plunged forward on to the book-rest.

In extenuation of this apparent laziness and irreverence, justice compels me to add that even the paid seats were generally so constructed as to make kneeling a positive torture. As all this may be set down to my imagination, I may as well say that kneeling used to be all but impossible at the Temple Church, the elevated foot-stools only permitting a lounging posture. This was considerably after the beautiful restoration of that church; but whether it is true now I do not know, as it is some years since I attended service there.

I might have mentioned any number of ordinary churches where the structural arrangements prohibited bodily worship, though there was every provision otherwise for the comfort of those who could afford the luxury of a pew. It is this condition of things which Newman must have had in mind when preaching his touching sermon on 'Worship a Preparation for Christ's Coming.'

The following passage goes direct to the point:

---

bolsters and pillows—and for these we love the Church! I will not guess what is done in them, who sits, stands, or lies asleep at prayers, communion, etc., but this I dare say, they are either to hide disorder or proclaim pride.'—See the Rev. J. E. Vaux on 'Church Folk-lore.'

'The season is chill and dark, and the breath of the morning is damp, and worshippers are few; but all this befits those who are by profession penitents and mourners, watchers and pilgrims.

'More dear to them that loneliness, more cheerful that severity, and more bright that gloom, than all those aids and appliances of luxury by which men nowadays attempt to make prayer less disagreeable to them. True faith does not covet comforts; it only complains when it is forbidden to kneel, when it reclines upon cushions, is protected by curtains, and encompassed by warmth. Its only hardship is to be hindered or to be ridiculed, when it would place itself as a sinner before its judge. They who realize that awful day when they shall see Him face to face, whose eyes are as a flame of fire, will as little bargain to *pray pleasantly* now as they will think of doing so then.'*

It was in October, 1840, that Macaulay's celebrated criticism on Von Ranke's 'History of the Popes' came out in the *Edinburgh Review*. We must make allowances for his rhetorical style; but there is a vast deal of truth in that passage in which he dilates on the *respectability* of the Established Church, as distinguishing it from Rome on the one hand, and from the sectaries on the other, and as largely accounting for its lost influence with the masses. After describing (rather flippantly) the conversion of a rough, uneducated man by a powerful sermon, or some such agency, Macaulay says:

'For a man thus minded, there is within the pale of the Establishment no place. He has been at no college, he cannot construe a Greek author or write a Latin theme, and he is told that, if he remains in the communion of the Church, he must do so as a hearer, and that, if he is resolved to be a teacher, he must begin by being a schismatic. His choice is soon made. He harangues on Tower Hill or in Smithfield. A congregation is formed; a

* 'Parochial and Plain Sermons,' vol. v.

license is obtained; a plain brick building, with a desk and benches, is run up, and named Ebenezer or Bethel. In a few weeks the Church has lost for ever a hundred families, not one of which entertained the least scruple about her articles, her liturgy, her government, or her ceremonies. Far different is the policy of the Church of Rome,' etc.

There was little provision in the Church of England for the poor and uneducated. For their children there was even less: the services seemed as if designed to repel rather than to attract them. Children's services, bright, cheerful, musical, were not yet; the children's sermon was not invented. Perched up in dangerous galleries, listening to tedious sermons, their condition was truly pitiable. And their minds were kept on the rack by the haunting presence of that awful functionary in gold-banded hat and uniform, armed with a far-reaching malacca cane—that ecclesiastical policeman known as the beadle. In those hot and crowded galleries the sun used to burn them by day and the gas by night. By the way, the gas was always under globes of ground-glass in those days, the effect of which on youthful eyes was wholly to induce slumber. If any of my hearers are troubled with insomnia, let me recommend them to fix their eyes on a lamp-globe while a dull sermon is being read to them. The effect is as soothing as any lullaby sung to restless infant.

I do not care to be autobiographical, but it may be interesting to mention the churches I attended in childhood. They were chiefly St. Peter's, Walworth, St. Mark's, Kennington, and St. Mary's, Newington, all important parish churches, all churches of one type, in which the features I have mentioned were well illustrated. Each had its beadle in uniform, its three-decker pulpit, its high pews, free seats, and diminutive communion-table with the usual appendages. And the services were of one type also. The Psalms were usually said in alternate verses by the minister and people, the latter led by a clerk whose education had been neglected, to whom the hard words were a sad stumbling-block. The clerks, by the way, were often a difficulty to the clergy with whom they officiated, and I am reminded of a story told by a curate who kindly proposed to educate his clerk in the matter of pronunciation. It is scarcely necessary to say that the offer was declined, with the suggestive remark: 'Why, sir, if I was to pronounce my words like you do, there would be no difference between us!'

I do not think there could be a better key to the general position than the hymn-books then in vogue. Of course, a free use was made of that collection by Tate and Brady characterized by Bishop Wilberforce as a *Dry Psalter*, and the hymns themselves, with a few noble exceptions, were scarcely so good as the metrical version of the Psalms. They were almost entirely of an Old Testament type; and while there were a great many allusions to the Omnipotent Creator, the spacious firmament, to Zion and Canaan, and so on, the person and character of Jesus Christ, to say nothing of the Christian Church and her functions, were sadly neglected. I must admit that some of the exceptional hymns to which I have referred are very beautiful, and their merit has led to their preservation in modern collections. But in nearly all hymns, whether good or bad, the *subjective* character prevailed; that is, their drift and purpose was to give expression to the spiritual state of the believer, rather than to fix his devotion on an external object of worship.

Most of these things, or of their most objectionable features, have passed away. So great and so general has been the change, that it would surprise us exceedingly if we were to come upon a church now of the type I have described, as we may occasionally in some out-of-the-way village in Ireland, or even in rural England, too remote or too isolated to be affected by the march of time. But less than fifty years ago the description I have given would be applicable to every church in town and country except those marked places where the dangerous principles of the Oxford Revivalists had found an entrance. Even there the outward signs of the most advanced teaching were below the ritual average of the present day.

One is sorry to add that the condition of the cathedrals was scarcely more encouraging than that of ordinary parish churches. I can remember going to St. Paul's in Dean Milman's time, to the Sunday afternoon service. The nave and space under the dome were unused, except on such grand occasions as the annual gathering of the charity children, when country visitors were, of course, prepared to forego the quiet ambulatory they usually afforded. The ordinary daily and Sunday services were carried on in the choir, then shut in by enormous iron grills, which practically made a separate chapel of it. Scholar and theologian though the Dean undoubtedly was, good Churchman though he was in a literary sense, the cathedral never rose in his time much beyond the level of an interesting historical monument. Things were pretty much the same at Westminster Abbey, and, in fact, at most cathedrals and collegiate churches throughout the country. Their condition, of course, varied with the status of their respective governing bodies. Many of the leading clergy had high ideals individually; but the ecclesiastical *Zeitgeist* sat as a blight on the land, and it was hard to rise above the prevailing tone. The architectural 'repairs and beautifyings' of the time strike us with amazement—the outward and visible signs of the absent grace. It would fill a large volume to describe the structural incongruities and mutilations which our cathedrals and other fine churches underwent during the religious siesta of the last and present century, not at all owing to narrowness of funds or unwillingness to spend them, but simply to the prevailing ignorance of ecclesiastical art. I can only just refer to the subject here. It must in justice be added that the sudden revival of Gothic art consequent on, or contemporaneous with, the spread of the Oxford opinions was attended with a reaction against all forms of art *but* Gothic, and this reaction resulted in many architectural mistakes as absurd as those it displaced. But I must not dwell on a subject which will fall into its proper place in a subsequent lecture.

To go back for a moment to the cathedral service, it was notorious that the lay-clerks by whom it was rendered—excellent fellows in their way—were chosen almost entirely on their musical qualifications; and provided a man had a captivating voice, especially that known as a 'cathedral bass' or a 'real alto' (as distinguished from falsetto), it mattered little what language he used, or what company he kept, much less whether he ever said his prayers or received the Holy Communion. The self-conceit of such choirmen as were chosen solely for their voices was notorious. The stereotyped phrase, 'Let us sing to the praise and glory of God,' which preceded the announcement of the hymn was too frequently a falsehood, the music evidently being to the praise and glory of the singers. If the Minor Canon happened to be musical, the choir would just tolerate him; if not, he was despised or ignored. There is a story of a choirman who even claimed precedence of the clergy on the authority of the Jewish ritual. When asked for chapter and verse, he would quote Psa. lxviii. 25, his reading of which was, 'The singers go before, the *ministers* follow after,' etc.

It was amusing, in spite of its irreverence, to see the choir coming into service sometimes, lounging up the nave in a straggling procession, the hinder ones putting on steam to catch up to those in front, adjusting their surplices as they went, hideous garbs flung over trousers of various patterns and colours unconcealed by cassocks. The chief features in the services were, of course, the anthem and the arrangement of the Canticles, technically known as a *service* delicious as musical performances, but utterly impossible to be joined in by the congregation.

Snuff and acid-drops are harmless things enough in their way, but it *was* rather objectionable to see the choir indulging in them openly during the sermon and lessons, with amiable courtesy passing them on to others who were unprovided with those delicacies. And it was still more objectionable to see the lounging and irreverent attitudes assumed during some of the most solemn parts of the service, although one must do cathedral choirs the justice to say that they knelt as a rule, according to the rubrical directions, while the congregations sat or bent forward in the way previously described. The sermon, of course, afforded the best opportunity for an easy lounge; and if it was more tedious than usual, there was a temptation to transmit messages of a humorous nature, or to make facetious marginal notes in the music-books. I have seen such altered titles of hymn-tunes as ' No. 4, Miles Lane,' and ' I'm nearer my God than Joe Robinson.'

These were signs of the general laxity. In the case of the professor of religion, there was the inevitable result of familiarity with sacred things when not restrained by a religious spirit. This, we know, is not peculiar to any time; but when everybody is lax the professional chorister or clergyman will be tempted to go beyond other people, partly in consequence of the monotonous repetition of tedious duties, partly out of a dread of hypocrisy. In the latter case he will often *assume* an outward irreverence against his natural inclination.

Perhaps, however, there was less excuse on this ground than we are generously inclined to allow, for it seems that the cathedral authorities were not generally very rigid about the attendance of their choristers. The boys were, of course, bound to attend, and where they lived under a common roof in the neighbourhood of the Cathedral there was no difficulty in the matter. The men, however, with or without the system of deputizing, seem to have had a pretty easy time of it. Even as recently as the time when the present Dean of St. Paul's first assumed office at the Cathedral we find him calling the choir together after service, and publicly remonstrating with certain members for irregular attendance. They had been in the habit of coming and going pretty much as they pleased. And I was told that when Dr. Bridge resumed the weekly choir-practice at the Abbey, which had fallen into abeyance during the latter part of Dr. Turle's time, there was a deal of grumbling among the lay-clerks at the hardship.

But times have changed. Most of these things have passed away, and with them possibly much that had better have been retained.

It was to an inherent spirit of religion, though concealed under such appearances as I have described, it was to a religious *soul*, so to speak, that such revivals as those of Wesley and Whitefield were able to appeal and owed their success. It was to this, too, that the Oxford Movement appealed.

English people, though very just and very generous, when once convinced of the genuineness of the cause which appeals to those qualities, are also very conservative by nature. Though the traditions, the inherited religion, of the opening years of this century were not the most ancient, they were nevertheless sufficiently venerable to make it extremely difficult to displace them. In the popular mind the Church of England dated no further back than Henry VIII. Luther, Cranmer, Ridley, and Hooper were names revered as saints or demi-gods; and in their natural devotion to the Reformation and its martyrs people forgot that their Church had a far higher antiquity, a nobler genealogy, and a more Catholic theology than the Reformation could show.

When, therefore, the Tractarians recalled attention to older doctrines, it is not at all wonderful that the general public were surprised and alarmed. The prevailing ignorance, and the absence of any systematic teaching to the contrary, were quite sufficient to account for the popular misconception of the aims and objects of those writers.*

But one *is* surprised *now* at the bishops of the time and the authorities at Oxford, who must have been aware that the doctrines brought forward were no 'fond thing vainly imagined,' but rested on a line of authority from St. John and St. Paul to St. Augustine, from St. Augustine to Bishops Bull and Pearson, from these to Burton and Van Mildert.

The tract-writers, as I have said, had a deep religious principle to appeal to, which in the long run has done them justice. At the time of their writing, however, this principle, or religious instinct, acted in two directions. While, on the one hand, it was open to receive the sublime ethical

* The following passage from one of Dr. Newman's sermons, though unfortunately more or less true at all times, was specially applicable to the time when it was written. 'Many a man gathers up, here and there, some fragments of religious knowledge. He hears one thing said in church, he sees another thing in the Prayer-Book; and among religious people, or in the world, he gains something more. In this way he gets possession of sacred words and statements, knowing very little about them really. He interprets them, as it may happen, according to the various and inconsistent opinions which he has met with, or he puts his own meaning upon them—that is, the meaning, as must needs be, of an untaught, not to say a carnal and irreverent mind. How can a man expect he shall discern and apprehend the real meaning and language of Scripture if he has never approached it as a learner, and waited on the Divine Author of it for the gift of wisdom? By continual meditation on the sacred text, by diligent use of the Church's instruction, he will come to understand what the Gospel doctrines are; but, most surely, if all the knowledge he has be gathered from a sentence caught up here, and an argument heard there, even when he is most orthodox in word, he has but a collection of phrases, on which he puts, not the right meaning, but his own meaning. And the least reflection must show you what a very poor and unworthy meaning, or, rather, how false a meaning "the natural man" will put upon "the things of the Spirit of God."'—'Parochial and Plain Sermons,' Sermon xii., vol. iii.

teaching of the rising school (which forms, for instance, such a conspicuous feature in Dr. Newman's sermons), and would possibly be led on to think that men who spoke so profoundly on subjects which it could appreciate might be equally well-informed on the abstruser doctrinal questions which then had all the appearance of novelty, it might occur to a reader unacquainted with the sincerity of the writers that the philosophical and highly moral tone was assumed, with jesuitical cleverness, as a mask to conceal, and as a vehicle to communicate, 'unsound' teaching. The fact is, that in those days, in the eyes of what was regarded as the religious portion of the community, everything which was not what is popularly called *Evangelical* was *unsound*.

The fashionable and popular religious literature of the day will show what I mean in a moment.

The books on everyone's table, ranking next to the Family Bible, were the fore-mentioned Hervey's 'Meditations,' Baxter's 'Saints' Rest,' Abbott's 'Way to do Good' and 'Young Christian,' Bunyan's immortal 'Pilgrim's Progress,' Legh Richmond's 'Dairyman's Daughter' and 'Young Cottager,' with perhaps Wesley's beautiful collection of hymns. Now, pray do not understand me as in any way disparaging these and such-like works. Some of them will last as long as the English language, and one and all laid great stress on the necessity and blessedness of personal religion. They did a vast deal of good in their generation, and I am sorry that people have left off reading most of them. But the defect in these excellent books, from the Anglo-Catholic point of view, was that they were almost entirely *subjective*. They take little or no account of the Church as an organized and visible society; they attach little importance to its distinctive doctrines. In fact, with these writers the term 'Church' simply meant all people who 'called themselves Christians.' Whatever religious body they attached themselves to, whatever the articles of their belief, were matters of secondary importance, provided they had the gift of faith, had been what is called *saved* or *converted*, said their prayers, and led good lives. But besides these things, it is obvious that there is an *objective* side to religion; that, independently of personal feelings and emotions, there is 'the faith once delivered to the saints'—a society to whose custody that faith has been entrusted, not merely a spiritual and invisible society, but visible and organized, with its head and succession of officers, its creeds and ceremonies. The main object of the Oxford writers was to remind the English Church that this faith was hers, that she was part of this universal or Catholic Church, and not merely the creation of Henry VIII. or Edward VI.; that she had higher doctrines and higher authority for them than those of the reformers of the Renaissance, or the popular preachers and writers of the day.

Bishop Wilberforce, a cautious observer of the movement, sometimes friendly, sometimes critical, was keenly alive to the danger of the time, and the need for an antidote. Speaking of the popular tendency, he says: 'It is the error of the earlier mystic, without his redeeming features of abstraction from the world and intense devotion.' 'How much healthier,' he goes on, 'is the tone of the true-hearted man, who from his cell in Saxony raised his voice indeed against the errors of the Popish system, but who could not bear the jargon which teaches us to attain high ends by throwing off the only means of reaching them! With homely earnestness he charges on the devil the delusion which, continually crying, "Spirit! Spirit! Spirit!" destroys the while all roads, bridges, scaling-ladders, and paths by which the Spirit can enter—namely, the visible order established by God in Holy Baptism, in outward forms, and in His own Word.'*

This was strictly in accordance with the teaching of the Tractarians. 'They had preached' (Dean Church observes)

---

* Introduction to 'Eucharistica.'

'that the Church of England, with all its Protestant feeling, and all its Protestant acts and history, was yet, as it professed to be, part and parcel of the great historic Catholic Church which had framed the Creeds, which had continued the Sacraments, which had preached and taught out of the Bible, which had given us our immemorial prayers. They had spared no pains to make out this great commonplace from history and theology; nor had they spared pains, while insisting on this dominant feature in the English Church, to draw strongly and broadly the lines which distinguished it from Rome.'*

* 'Oxford Movement,' chap. xv.

LECTURE II.

PRECURSORS OF THE REVIVAL.

THE opening words of Schiller's 'Thirty Years' War' are familiar to most readers. He says: 'From the beginning of the religious war in Germany to the peace at Münster, hardly anything great and remarkable has happened in the political world of Europe in which the Reformation has not had the principal share.' We might go further, and say that scarcely *any* important event has happened since the Reformation which has not been affected, directly or indirectly, by that movement. Especially is this true of subsequent religious transactions on a large scale, whether in Roman Catholic or Protestant countries. But the divergence of their followers from the lines of the original actors in that important drama is very striking. It is curious, for instance, to observe that the modern German critical school, which undoubtedly owes its existence to the teaching of Martin Luther, has proceeded to deny the personal existence of the devil, which was perhaps more of a reality to the great Reformer than it has been to any other human being since the times of the New Testament. On the other hand, many subsequent thinkers, though belonging to religious bodies which derive their origin, or, at least, much of their character, from the Reformation, living at a time remote from the immediate subjects of controversy, have been able to take a calmer and less prejudiced view of the questions at issue, and have *gone back*, as we should say, from the principles of their founders. Hence the study of the Reformation leads people in two opposite directions, which we may call liberal and conservative.

Disregarding temporary and local opinions, the latter has, in the main, been the effect of the Reformation on the great body of English writers and English theology. There have, of course, been distinguished scholars on the extreme Protestant side; but, taking English thinkers and writers as a whole, from the time of Elizabeth to the present day—those, that is, of sufficient calibre to be regarded as *classical*—we shall find that the weight of their authority has been, I will not say exactly counter to the Reformation, but of a distinctly moderating tendency. At the time of the Oxford Revival such writers happened to be temporarily out of favour; they were not read. This is the best explanation of the ignorance, not only among the general public, but in high ecclesiastical quarters, of the real object of the leaders of the movement. It has become perfectly clear since, though it was not at all clear to their contemporaries, that they were not stating new or foreign doctrine, but merely reviving what was neglected, as *they* thought, to the detriment of the English Church and the religious life of the country. It will help us to enter into this view of the case if we look into any of the 'Tracts for the Times,' or other publications of the same writers. We shall find that the doctrines therein resuscitated are usually of such a commonplace and self-evident character as scarcely to need insisting upon; and it will be a matter of extreme surprise to most of us that statements so harmless, and in the main so true, should have created the sensation and alarm which we know resulted from their publication.

The fact is, if it has done nothing else (and that it has done a great deal more I hope to show as we go on), the Oxford Movement has so far stimulated inquiry and historical research, that the main points for which its leaders contended are now recognised as established truths—not merely private and obscure opinions, but such as have been substantiated by a consensus of historians and theologians of the highest standing. It is rather for their bold and unconventional treatment of old, than for the invention of new subjects, that the credit of originality is due to the Oxford writers.*

I am prepared to admit that, as in the case of the Reformation, the followers of the Oxford Movement have frequently gone beyond its originators. This happens with *all* movements. They must necessarily be in one direction; and a great party naturally attracts to it inferior spirits, who are hurried along with the current without themselves carrying sufficient ballast to steady their progress. Newman's words on this point are worth quoting: 'There will ever be a number of persons professing the opinions of a move-

* 'Our present state of peril is the result of a continuous and lengthened effort which has been maintained by the leaders of the Romanizing party in the Church, with unwearied diligence, now for nearly twenty years. Perhaps it might be said that the seeds of it have been lying dormant from the period of the Reformation. Popery in the seventh and subsequent centuries was but the development of that mystery of iniquity which was working in the Apostles' days. The Romanizing principles of the present day are in like manner the resuscitation of that smouldering Pharisaism and overweening love of forms and ceremonies and Church authority *which have ever pervaded a large portion of the Church of England.* It is but the calling into life and active energy that deep-seated dislike to the truth as it is in Jesus, and to the distinctive doctrines of grace, which the Apostle describes as "the carnal mind, which is enmity against God."'—'An Appeal to the Evangelical Members of the Church of England in reference to the present Crisis,' by Daniel Wilson, M.A., Vicar of Islington.

I give this extract from a pamphlet published in 1850 by an opponent of the movement. It shows that even from his point of view the doctrines of the Tractarians were tolerably old; and if we substitute Catholic for Roman, and so on, it is pretty much such an account as a friend might have written, except, of course, the condemnation of the doctrines involved; but even this is interesting, as showing what was thought of them at the time.

ment party, who talk loudly and strangely, do odd or fierce things, display themselves unnecessarily, and disgust other people; persons too young to be wise, too generous to be cautious, too warm to be sober, or too intellectual to be humble. Such persons will be very apt to attach themselves to particular persons, to use particular names, to say things merely because others do, and to act in a party-spirited way.'*

It is unfair, therefore, to charge back on the leaders of any movement the excesses or failings of their successors, as if these were necessarily involved, and contained, as it were, in embryo, in their teaching. It would be as unfair, for instance, to blame Dr. Pusey for all the extravagant and meaningless ritual one meets with, as to make Luther responsible for the scepticism and infidelity of modern Germany.

The Tractarians had great precedents for what they said, and it is of their precursors that I propose to speak this evening. As I said in my first lecture, there has been a great line of writers in the English Church on whose theology the Oxford Tracts were based, and who substantially corroborate their view of the Church as a society, and of its separate doctrines. Of course, the Anglo-Catholic teaching varied in degree according to the peculiarities of individual writers, and varied still more at different periods. Thus, the writers of the *sixteenth* century, more immediately affected by the Reformation, were necessarily more emphatic in their denunciations of what is called *Popery* than those of the *seventeenth* century. But it would be a great mistake to suppose that the latter had nothing to say against it. The Caroline theologians were distinct *Anglicans*, and many of them wrote and acted very decidedly against the errors of Rome. For instance, Bishop Taylor wrote a 'Dissuasive against Popery,' and his other writings abound

* Article on 'The State of Religious Parties,' published originally in the *British Critic*, for April, 1839, and quoted in 'The Apologia.'

with matter to the same purpose. Dr. Brevint, though he was not Protestant enough to prevent his expulsion by the Parliamentary visitors, was, as he tells us, 'acquainted with every corner of that' (the Roman) 'Church.' His principal works, in fact, are 'The Mystery of the Roman Mass laid open,' 'Saul and Samuel at Endor; or, The New Ways of Service and Salvation which tempt Men to Rome truly represented and refuted.' There were also certain Latin works of his exposing Roman corruptions. On the other hand, there is his book on 'The Christian Sacrament and Sacrifice,' republished in 1739, on the high recommendation of it by Bishop Waterland in his Charge.

It is a well-known incident that when Dr. Patrick and Dr. Jane (neither ultra-Protestants) were challenged to defend their faith against two Roman priests in the presence of James II., the King went off in a rage during the contest, saying that he 'never heard a bad cause so well defended. His Majesty made various attempts to draw Patrick over to the Romish Church, but the Dean (as he then was) was immovable. The Caroline writers, in short, held the position since defined as the *Via Media*. They perhaps understood the controversy with Rome better than any other set of men, before or since, and were clearly opposed to Romish error; but where they differed from the reformers of the previous century was just in this point: that whereas the earlier set of men (very excusably) were not alive to the necessity of a Church as a visible and organized society, the latter *were*. Or perhaps it would be more correct to say that the opinion of the early reformers about the Church was like Coleridge's on the subject of ghosts: they had seen too much to believe.

It is not at all to be wondered at, on the whole, that, their views of the Church and the Christian priesthood being almost identical, the Oxford writers should be full of allusions to, and quotations from, their precursors of the seventeenth century. 'It was true,' Newman remarks, 'that

I held a large bold system of religion, very unlike the Protestantism of the day; but it was the concentration and adjustment of the statements of great Anglican authorities, and I had as much right to hold it as the Evangelical, and more right than the Liberal, party could show, for asserting their own respective doctrines. As I declared on occasion of Tract XC., I claimed in ;behalf of who would in the Anglican Church the right of holding, with Bramhall, a comprecation with the Saints, and the Mass all but Transubstantiation, with Andrewes; or with Hooker, that Transubstantiation itself is not a point for Churches to part communion upon; or with Hammond, that a General Council, truly such, never did, never shall, err in a matter of faith; or with Bull, that man had in paradise, and lost on the fall, a supernatural habit of grace; or with Thorndike, that penance is a propitiation for post-baptismal sin; or with Pearson, that the all-powerful name of Jesus is no otherwise given than in the Catholic Church.'*

It is a very striking feature of the movement (at all events in its later stages), that a revival was induced by it, not only of the Caroline *theology*, but also of the *secular history* of that interesting period. I hope to refer to this later on, when we come to the literature of the movement. Suffice it to say here that several charming little historical stories dealing with the fortunes of Cavaliers and Roundheads were an indirect result of the controversy, in which the sympathies of Churchmen were enlisted on behalf of the Stuart family and their adherents as representing the Church of England in its contest with Puritanism. As I said before, the teaching of the Caroline divines was carried on and extended by the Nonjurors, whose dispersion about the country was of course favourable to the spread of their opinions.

These opinions, political and religious, continued to be held here and there long after the extinction of the party

* 'Apologia,' ch. iii.

which propagated them. And the mere fact of men having had the courage to suffer deprivation for them was an inducement to others to think there was a good deal in them as being worth suffering for. Rightly or wrongly, the Nonjurors were invested with the credit of that secondary sort of martyrdom which consists in a *willingness* to die for one's belief. All this helped to keep alive in certain places that traditional *high* view of the Church which the Oxford school sought to revive and intensify, and accounts for the ready reception of their writings in quarters previously under Nonjuring influence. To use an illustration of Jeremy Taylor's, it is easy to rekindle a taper when the wick is still glowing.* Several of the Nonjurors were laymen, who, by by reason of their official position, were obliged to take the oath of allegiance to William and Mary or lose their places. These were, of course, of the same tone of Churchmanship as their priestly companions. The most distinguished of these laymen in a literary sense were Robert Nelson, author of the 'Fasts and Festivals,' still perhaps the best book of its kind for elementary religious teachers, and William Law, already mentioned as the author of the 'Serious Call.'

Among the illustrious laymen who have helped to perpetuate the Anglo-Catholic school of theology, I ought not to forget our good old friend Izaak Walton, best known by his 'Complete Angler,' but also known to readers as one of the most charming biographers in our language. His lives of Dr. Donne, Wotton, Hooker, George Herbert, and Sanderson show what he was himself from the Churchmen he admired, and whose doctrines he cordially shared. This book was a great favourite with Dr. Johnson (seven years

---

* Dean Burgon tells us that the father of Routh, of Magdalen, *always* preached in his surplice at his place in Suffolk. And I have heard that there are places where the Eucharistic vestments have never been abandoned. Dr. Lee, writing to the *Gentleman's Magazine* in 1863, says that "the primitive and patristic custom of reserving the Sacrament has never been entirely given up in the ancient Church of Scotland."

of age when Queen Anne came to the throne), who was also a thoroughgoing High Churchman of the old-fashioned type.*

There was much in Dr. Johnson's opinions which would have laid him open to censure at Oxford had he lived fifty years later. For instance, you will remember that one of the objectionable points in Tract XC. was the distinction drawn by the writer between the *Romish* doctrine of purgatory, which the 22nd Article condemns, and other possible doctrines of purgatory, which he said, as the Article does not mention, may consistently be held by those who sign it. Dr. Johnson goes a step further, and maintains that even the Romish doctrine of purgatory, unpopular as it was in Protestant England, was not so utterly illogical that nothing could be said for it. His conversation with Boswell on that and a few other controverted subjects is worth reading.

Boswell asks: 'What do you think, sir, of purgatory as believed by the Roman Catholics?' Johnson: 'Why, sir, it is a very harmless doctrine. They are of opinion that the generality of mankind are neither so obstinately wicked as to deserve everlasting punishment, nor so good as to merit being admitted into the society of blessed spirits, and, therefore, that God is graciously pleased to allow of a middle state, where they may be purified by certain degrees of suffering. You see, sir, there is nothing unreasonable in this.' Boswell: 'But, then, sir, their Masses for the dead?' Johnson: 'Why, sir, if it be once established that there are souls in purgatory, it is as proper to pray for *them* as for our brethren of mankind who are yet in this life.' Boswell: 'The idolatry of the Mass?' Johnson: 'Sir, there is no

* There was, as is well known, a very interesting High Church revival in Queen Anne's time, which is worth a separate study. In this connexion I cannot help mentioning the numerous week-day services in the City churches, as given in Paterson's 'Pietas Londinensis,' which should be compared with the record of 'Daily Prayers in and about the City,' quoted from a book of 1683 in No. 84 of 'Tracts for the Times.'

idolatry in the Mass. They believe God to be there, and they adore Him.' Boswell: 'The worship of saints?' Johnson: 'Sir, they do not worship saints; they invoke them. They only ask their prayers. I am talking all this time of the *doctrines* of the Church of Rome. I grant you that, in *practice*, purgatory is made a lucrative imposition, and the people do become idolatrous, as they recommend themselves to the tutelary protection of particular saints. I think their giving the sacrament only in one kind is criminal, because it is contrary to the express institution of Christ, and I wonder how the Council of Trent admitted it.' Boswell: 'Confession?' Johnson: 'Why, I don't know but that is a good thing. The Scripture says, "Confess your faults one to another," and the priests confess as well as the laity. Then it must be considered that their absolution is only upon repentance, and often upon penance also. You think your sins may be forgiven without penance upon repentance alone.'

The fact is, Johnson was a believer in the *Via Media*. When arguing with Romanists, he could doubtless have given them first-rate reasons for being an Anglican, as his biographer implies a few lines further on. But, like the Tractarians, he seems to have thought that the Roman Church was not so hopelessly bad, nor the English Church so perfect as was popularly supposed. We cannot read Boswell's fascinating biography without seeing that the doctor was a devout member of the Anglo-Catholic Church, and believed in her position between Rome on the one hand and the various forms of dissent on the other. His observance of Good Friday is worth noticing by nineteenth-century Churchmen. His touching and cautiously-worded prayers on the occasion of his wife's death are also interesting as throwing light on his ideas about the intermediate state.*

---

* 'On the 9th of April (1773), being Good Friday, I breakfasted with him on tea and cross buns, *Doctor* Levett, as Frank called him, making the tea. He carried me with him to the church of St. Clement Danes,

Dr. Johnson died in 1784, but before he passed away a literary constellation was appearing on the horizon, whose influence, as preparatory to the Oxford Movement, has hardly received sufficient recognition. I refer to the great 'Wizard of the North,' Sir Walter Scott, and that group of writers who were contemporaneous with him, and who, from the circumstance of their common residence in the Lake district, have been classified together in a single school. This classification is somewhat arbitrary, for though

---

where he had his seat, and his behaviour was, as I had imagined to myself, solemnly devout. I shall never forget the tremulous earnestness with which he pronounced the awful petition in the Litany: "In the hour of death, and in the day of judgment, good Lord deliver us." We went to church both in the morning and evening. In the interval between the two services *we did not dine*, but he read in the Greek New Testament, and I turned over several of his books.' One of these books, Boswell adds, was Archbishop Laud's Diary. — Boswell's 'Life of Johnson.'

'*April* 26th, 1752, being after 12 at night of the 25th.—O Lord, Governor of heaven and earth, in whose hands are embodied and departed spirits, if Thou hast ordained the souls of the dead to minister to the living, and appointed my departed wife to have care of me, grant that I may enjoy the good effects of her attention and ministration, whether exercised by appearance, impulses, dreams, or in any other manner agreeable to Thy government. Forgive my presumption, enlighten my ignorance, and however meaner agents are employed, grant me the blessed influences of Thy Holy Spirit, through Jesus Christ our Lord. Amen.'

'*March* 28, 1753.—I kept this day as the anniversary of my Tetty's death, with prayers and tears in the morning. In the evening I prayed for her conditionally, if it were lawful.'—*Ibid.*

On looking over the collection of Dr. Johnson's prayers, published at the end of his works, I find the following intercessions for the departed, which are even more pointed than the above:

'I commend, O Lord, so far as it may be lawful, into Thy hands the soul of my departed mother, beseeching Thee to grant her whatsoever is most beneficial to her in her present state.'—*January* 23, 1759.

'Almighty God, who art the giver of all good, enable me to remember with due thankfulness the comforts and advantages which I have enjoyed by the friendship of Henry Thrale, for whom, so far as is lawful, I humbly implore Thy mercy in his present state.'—*June* 22, 1781.

the writers had much in common, especially in classical elegance and purity of style, there was a marked individuality in each case; and, in fact, we frequently find them criticising and disputing with each other on points of doctrine, literary and ecclesiastical. Any coincidence of opinion among them on our particular subject will therefore be all the more interesting.

Their dates are as follows:

Sir Walter Scott	1771-1832
Samuel Taylor Coleridge	1772-1834
Robert Southey	1774-1843
William Wordsworth	1770-1850
Thomas De Quincey	1785-1859

Let us take them in order, and see if we can trace any sympathy between them and the Oxford writers.

Everyone knows that the Prayer-Book of the Scottish Episcopal Church, drawn up chiefly under the direction of Archbishop Laud, is even more in accord with the primitive liturgies, and has been less modified by Calvinistic influences than the English Book of Common Prayer. Sir Walter Scott was a devout member of the Scottish Episcopal Church, and accepted its Prayer-Book *con amore*. The positions of the Scottish and Irish Episcopal Churches are curiously reversed in their respective countries. Whereas in Ireland the Protestant Church seems driven to an excess of Protestantism by the proximity of the dominant Roman Catholic religion, the Church in Scotland seems forced into as strong a contrast as possible with the Presbyterian and Puritan school, which holds the ruling position and State advantages in that country. Consequently the Scottish Episcopal Church has all along exhibited more of the Catholic and less of the Protestant character, not only than the sister Church in Ireland, but even than the Church of England, where the distinction between one school and another has not been so necessary. It is not at all wonderful, therefore, that the Oxford writers were given to quoting the official documents of the Scottish Church as a precedent for what they sought to revive in England; and that the leading Scottish Churchmen were more sympathetic, or at least less antagonistic, to the movement than their brethren south of the Tweed.

The Scottish Church, like the English, has been *raised* by the movement; but, as a matter of fact, the Scottish Church in 1833 was in much the same position as it took the Church of England twenty or thirty years to attain. Of course I mean *doctrinally*, for outward ceremonial, the natural outcome of the Catholic Revival, was scarcely touched; it formed no part of the object of the revivalists. Doctrinally, then, there was much sympathy between the Scotch Episcopalians and the Oxford men. Sir Walter Scott was what we should call an old-fashioned High Churchman and Tory, for politics and churchmanship in his day, as for long afterwards, seemed inseparably allied. He died in 1832, the year before the movement assumed a definite shape, and consequently says nothing directly about it; but his churchmanship being what it was, we shall look in vain through his writings and recorded sayings for anything that can be construed into an argument against the general teaching of the movement, while we shall find very much in support and anticipation of it. The whole tenor of his writings is of that elevated and liberal type that we may rightly call *Catholic*, and contains nothing likely to bring ridicule on Catholic doctrine and practice. And there are certain specific works of his distinctly tending to break down misconceptions about the pre-Reformation Church, which was so unpopular in the Protestant mind, but which, after all, was still a part of that universal system with which the revivalists sought to identify the Church of England. The Church of the Middle Ages lives again in such poems as 'Marmion,' 'Rokeby,' 'The Lord of the Isles,' and 'The Lay of the Last Minstrel.' It would be hard to beat some of the writer's cathedral scenes—such, for instance, as the description of Melrose by moonlight. Milton's celebrated meditation in 'Il Penseroso' may be finer; but in this case it is a solitary instance of appreciation wrung from the writer, as it were, by a momentary triumph of the poet over the Puritan, whereas Scott is all through full of a steady enthusiasm for what was really admirable in the Dark Ages, as they are called. His strong antiquarian and historical sympathies led him to take a fairer view of the past. But it was not merely a love of old architecture and old legends; he showed his readers that there was much real beauty in the older ceremonial. I don't think there are any finer descriptions than he gives us of religious processions or the mediæval services. And what is more, he shows us that the pre-Reformation Church was capable of producing noble, chivalrous, humane, devout, and studious characters. 'Ivanhoe,' 'Count Robert of Paris,' and 'The Talisman' show us something distinctly favourable of the Church of the Crusaders; 'The Monastery' and 'The Abbot' enlist our sympathies with its fallen greatness during the Reformation. In Father Eustace, the hero of the latter story, we have a scholarly and saintly character, the natural product of Catholic training, but which Protestantism scarcely aims at and seldom produces. In short, in these romances Scott divests the ancient Church of her abuses or puts them in the background, to reveal what was stately in her worship and useful in her system. This was certainly in accord with the work of the revivers. They set themselves to prove that the Church of England was the ancient Church, minus her superstitions and corruptions, identical with her in system, orders, and fundamental doctrines.

Mediævalism and Reformation had each their effect on the Church, modifying its outward aspect and even its inner life; but after all they left its vital principles untouched— the Church of to-day was not cut off by any movement or phase of life from the Church of the past. Sir Walter Scott, I say, paved the way for the restoration of this doctrine, popularly ignored in the early part of this century—and he did it in the pleasantest manner possible—under the guise of poetry and romance.

I might also call your attention to his novels of the Royalist and Roundhead period, such as 'The Legend of Montrose,' 'Woodstock,' and 'Peveril of the Peak,' in which his sympathies are clearly with the former and the Church. These charming tales, as everybody knows, were eagerly read throughout the country, and prepared the public mind for a more definitely religious view of the points at issue between the Church and the sectaries, such as was afterwards set forth in certain romances and more serious works of the Oxford school. I am afraid that the Waverley novels are no longer read as they ought to be; but the effects of Scott's influence can perhaps better be gauged now than at the height of his popularity. Then it is quite possible it was merely the historical and literary power of his writings that was felt; but men can scarcely ever get attached to any period of the past, through any of its features, without developing a taste for other features. The historical and antiquarian interest would tend to create a doctrinal and moral interest, and in this way a novel may do the work of a sermon without the reader being conscious of its influence. Anyhow, a friend has told me that his first serious impressions about the Church were due to his reading the Waverley novels at an age when he was incapable of analyzing his thoughts.

Before leaving this part of our subject I should just like to call your attention to Scott's love of the old hymns of the Latin Church, in which he seems to have anticipated Dr. Neale and other translators. We have a little specimen of his work in a version of the 'Dies Iræ,' published in Hymns Ancient and Modern.*

Those who agree with the view of Scott's influence suggested above will not be surprised to hear that when

* No. 206, 'That Day of Wrath.'

Lockhart's 'Life of Scott' came out, John Keble wrote a review of it in the *British Critic*, full of loving sympathy with its great subject, and valuable at this day as containing Keble's judgment on the true objects and principles of poetry. There was evidently a poetical and religious connecting link between Abbotsford and Hursley.

To be strictly chronological, I ought to have taken Wordsworth before Scott, as he was born in the previous year, but I thought it would be better to consider the lake-writers together in deference to the received classification. Those who have not read Coleridge's 'Biographia Literaria' I would strongly advise to do so, for various reasons, but chiefly at present because it contains in its twenty-second chapter a masterly analysis of Wordsworth's poetry, of which the defects and excellencies are carefully illustrated by quotations.

We must admit that whatever influence Scott has exerted on the mind of this century is due to his prose romances. His poetry, though not destitute here and there of fire, is too tame on the whole for modern readers. It was when Byron, with his fiery genius and disregard of grammar, burst upon the scene that Scott took to the species of prose in which he excels, and it is a good thing for society that he did so. Wordsworth holds a middle place between the tameness of Scott and the licentiousness of Byron. He combines some of the qualities of both. There is all the religious seriousness of Scott, but it is lifted out of the conventional groove. There is at least as much command of language within the writer's chastened lines of thought as Byron exhibits, but it is refined by the restrictions of his conscience and a delicate sense of accuracy in adjusting words to their meaning. The result is that many readers who find Scott's verses too dull, and who have scruples about Byron's morality, are drawn to Wordsworth. They find in him both a religious and a linguistic satisfaction. In short, he answers to the wants of the great body of

English readers. He rose in the nick of time to show that religious and philosophical poetry need not be tedious, and his influence on English thought and taste has been immense.

It would be an exaggeration to count him pre-eminently as nature's poet. Though he drew much of his inspiration from nature, he drew quite as much from the recesses of his inner consciousness. And being pre-eminently a religious man and a philosopher, there is scarcely one of his poems, as he himself tells us, that does not direct attention to some moral sentiment or to some philosophical principle for the guidance of life. I have already said that the popular religion of England was strongly subjective. It is not surprising, therefore, that Wordsworth's poetry is largely the expression of his own thoughts and feelings, which are, of course, typical of the thoughts and feelings of many other people. On the other hand, his fondness for nature takes him frequently out of himself, and we must credit him with raising the religious taste of his day from excessive introspection to the contemplation of external objects. We see here much in common between him and the author of the 'Christian Year,' and when in 1839 he visited Oxford to take up his doctorate, he received the heartfelt welcome from his brother poet which left such a precious impression on his memory.

Although Keble was indebted to Bishop Ken for the general plan of his work, he owed to Wordsworth much of that appreciation of nature, doubtless also some of that felicity of expression, which is so marked a feature in both writers. The principles on which they worked being alike, we shall not be surprised to find an interesting doctrinal agreement, a few instances of which I give below.* I may

* 'Twenty years ago, roaming one day (as so often I did) with our immortal Wordsworth, I took the liberty of telling him, at a point of our walk where nobody could possibly overhear me, unless it were old Father Helvellyn, that I feared his theological principles were not quite

remind you that Wordsworth's 'Excursion' was published in 1814, his 'Ecclesiastical Sonnets' appeared in 1820, and Keble's 'Christian Year' in 1827.

---

so sound as his friends would wish. They wanted tinkering a little. But, what was worse, I did not see how they *could* be tinkered in the particular case which prompted my remark; for in that place to tinker, or in any respect to alter, was to destroy. It was a passage in the "Excursion," where the Solitary had described the baptismal rite as washing away the taint of original sin, and, in fact, working the effect which is called technically *regeneration*. In the "Excursion" this view was advanced, not as the poet's separate opinion, but as the avowed doctrine of the English Church, to which Church Wordsworth and myself yielded gladly a filial reverence. But *was* this the doctrine of the English Church? *That* I doubted; and, judging by my own casual experience, I fancied that a considerable majority in the Church gave an interpretation to this sacrament, differing by much from that in the "Excursion." Wordsworth was startled and disturbed at hearing it whispered, even before Helvellyn, who is old enough to keep a secret, that his theology might possibly limp a little. I, on my part, was not sure that it *did*, but I feared so; and as there was no chance that I should be murdered for speaking freely (though the place was lonely and the evening getting dusky, and W. W. had a natural resemblance to Mrs. Ratcliffe's Schedoni and other assassins roaming through prose and verse), I stood to my disagreeable communication with the courage of a martyr. The question between us being one of mere fact (not what *ought* to be the doctrine, but what *was* the doctrine of our English Church at that time), there was no opening for much discussion, and, on Wordsworth's suggestion, it was agreed to refer the point to his learned brother, Dr. Christopher Wordsworth, just then meditating a visit to his native lakes. That visit in a short time "came off," and then, without delay, our dispute "came on" for judgment. I had no bets upon the issue; one can't bet with Wordsworth, and I don't know that I should have ventured to back myself in a case of that nature. However, I felt a slight anxiety on the subject, which was very soon and kindly removed by Dr. Wordsworth's deciding "sans phrase" that I, the original mover of the strife, was wrong, wrong as wrong could be, without an opening, in fact, to any possibility of being more wrong. To this decision I bowed at once.'—De Quincey on Protestantism.

The passage referred to, which occurs in the fifth book of the 'Excursion,' is as follows:

> 'And, when the pure
> And consecrating element hath cleansed

The mutual appreciation of Keble and Wordsworth is thus related in Sir J. T. Coleridge's 'Life of Keble.' He says :

> The original stain, the child is thus received
> Into the second ark, Christ's Church, with trust
> That he, from wrath redeemed, therein shall float
> Over the billows of this troublesome world
> To the fair land of everlasting life.'

The same doctrine is stated in other words in Wordsworth's little poem on baptism :

> 'Blest be the Church, that watching o'er the needs
> Of infancy, provides a timely shower,
> Whose virtue changes to a Christian flower
> The sinful product of a bed of weeds !'

It is scarcely necessary to say that Keble held the doctrine of baptismal regeneration in its fullest sense. It is briefly stated in his verses on 'Holy Baptism' in the 'Christian Year' :

> 'A few calm words of faith and prayer,
>   A few bright drops of holy dew,
> Shall work a wonder there
>   Earth's charmers never knew.'

There is no time for a detailed comparison between the poets, but I cannot refrain from quoting Wordsworth's exquisite lines on the Virgin, which go about as far as anything Keble ever wrote. They should be compared with his hymn on the Annunciation—'Ave Maria ! blessed Maid' :

> 'Mother ! whose virgin bosom was uncrost
> With the least shade of thought to sin allied ;
> Woman ! above all women glorified,
> Our tainted nature's solitary boast ;
> Purer than foam on central ocean tost ;
> Brighter than Eastern skies at daybreak strewn
> With fancied roses, than the unblemished moon
> Before her wane begins on heaven's blue coast ;
> Thy image falls to earth. Yet some, I ween,
> Not unforgiven the suppliant knee might bend,
> As to a visible power, in which did blend
> All that was mixed and reconciled in thee
> Of mother's love with maiden purity,
> Of high with low, celestial with terrene !'
>   'Ecclesiastical Sketches.'

'This (1810-11) was a period when the Lake Poets, as they were called, and especially Wordsworth and my uncle, had scarcely any place in the literature of the country, except as a mark for the satire of some real wits and some misnamed critics of considerable repute. I possessed—the gift of my uncle—the 'Lyrical Ballads' and 'Wordsworth's Poems' (these last in the first edition). It is among the pleasant recollections of my life that I first made the great poet known to Keble. As might have been expected, he read him with avidity. The admiration for his poetry, which he conceived in youth, never waned in after-life; indeed, when he came to know the man, it was augmented —I may rather say completed—by the respect and regard which his character inspired. It was hardly possible for Keble to be a very enthusiastic admirer of any poetry unless he had at least conceived a good opinion of the writer. I may say, in passing, that Wordsworth's admiration of the author of the 'Christian Year,' and the volume itself, was in after-life very warm. There were few of the many tributes which he received which he set a greater value on than the mention made of him by Keble in the Theatre at Oxford, when he received his honorary degree, and the dedication to him of the "Prælectiones."'

The history of the world is a history of reactions. Great movements occur from time to time with their disturbing effects; 'the fountains of the great deep are broken up.' Things settle down. A period of comparative calm is succeeded by a period of stagnation, till another social eruption happens, when the process of disturbance, chaos, settlement, peace, stagnation, is repeated. The years preceding the Oxford Revival were years of stagnation. The Reformation, the French Revolution, the Revival of Wesley, had come and gone; they had done their good and bad work. Men's minds had been terribly stirred by them. The excitement, not altogether unhealthy, ended, after the usual gradations, in a quiet which was unhealthy. This, in the natural and inevitable course of things, was to be succeeded by a fresh agitation.

The Oxford Movement was merely one manifestation of a mental activity which was making itself felt in various directions. The mutterings of thunder were heard in the air; volcanic action was going on below. There were signs of life and movement in the poetical, the religious, the social, the philosophical world. France had had its movements, Germany had had its movements, in each case determined by the character of the people of those countries. It was now England's turn.

From its insular position England is necessarily rather later than the rest of Europe in feeling, or at least in manifesting, the spirit of the age. As it was in the Renaissance, so it was now. But she could not remain for ever unaffected by forces which were exciting the rest of the thinking, civilized world. The great Samuel Taylor Coleridge had been educated in Germany, and had drunk deep at the fountains of German scepticism and German mysticism. He united in his own peculiar personality the poet, the mystic, and the philosopher. He was an English edition, so to speak, of Kant and Goethe. He did for England in his day what Carlyle has done since. He imported into English thought a vast deal from the land of Luther with which we should otherwise have been unacquainted. Goethe, Schiller, Kant, Luther himself, Lessing, and a host of others of whom Englishmen had little knowledge, were absorbed by Coleridge into his own somewhat chaotic mind, and given out again to English readers either in actual translation or in the modified form of Coleridge's philosophy.*

The contrast between him and Wordsworth is perhaps best illustrated by their mutual agreement to write a separate work simultaneously, each subject to be chosen by the

* Goethe was born in 1749, Kant in 1724, Lessing in 1729, and Schiller in 1759.

writer for himself as suitable to his particular genius. The result was Wordsworth's 'Excursion,' illustrating the force of simply natural objects on a natural and unsophisticated character, and Coleridge's 'Ancient Mariner,' which depended entirely on the 'Imagination.' The works were well chosen as typical of the cast of mind of each writer. These great men, so different, and yet in many points with such a strong affinity for each other, were both destined to play an important part in the religious phenomena of the time. In the year 1825 Coleridge published his remarkable 'Aids to Reflection,' in 1840 his 'Confessions of an Inquiring Spirit.'

These books were of a different stamp to anything that had yet appeared in England. There had been atheists, professedly such, there had been sneering sceptics; but there had been nothing between them and the orthodox apologists, whose works did duty as text-books for men in training for orders.*

Coleridge, while allowing the utmost liberty to the play of reason and intellect, while keeping his judgment open on matters which he thought incapable of solution, while weighing Church and Bible doctrines in the balances, and deciding upon them on their own merits instead of simply leaning on antiquity or authority, yet pursued all his investigation and criticism in a spirit of the deepest reverence. The distinguishing feature of his writings is a Catholic breadth of view. He is unfettered by the prejudices which

* Perhaps we may except Sir Thomas Browne's celebrated 'Religio Medici' (written in 1635), which seems to occupy a position between works distinctly hostile and those yielding unquestioning obedience to the received theology. But the 'Religio Medici,' as its name implies, is rather a collection of one man's opinions, with his personal motives for holding them, than an argumentative work for general use. It is too eccentric and subjective to be logical. In many points, however, it is anticipative of Coleridge, as well as of the Catholic and Broad Church position. The writer's independence led him in various directions.

it must be confessed give an appearance of bias to most writings, whether critical or apologetic. His conclusions, therefore, are always valuable, whether one agrees with them or not.

Coleridge's mind and Coleridge's writings were the result of a reaction against the insipid and unintellectual Protestantism of the eighteenth and early nineteenth century. In one sense he was the precursor of 'Essays and Reviews,' and the papers of 'Lux Mundi.' He also prepared the way for the Catholic Revival by clearing the air, forcing men to think, by asserting the rights of the intellect against the emotions, by breaking down a good deal of Protestant prejudice—*e.g.*, as regards the verbal inspiration of Scripture —the (entirely) spiritual character of the Church, the (entirely) commemorative nature of the Eucharist, and so on. Besides thus negatively serving the Catholic cause by the removal of certain prejudices likely to operate against it, his work was constructive ; and we find him laying down here and there the same doctrines as the revivalists were advocating—*e.g.*, where he advocates the united authority of the Bible and the Church : 'There are likewise sacred writings, which, *taken in connexion with the institution and perpetuity of a visible Church*, all believers revere as the most precious boon of God, next to Christianity itself, and attribute both their communication and preservation to an especial Providence.' Or in the following view of the Eucharist : 'After this course of study you may then take up and peruse sentence by sentence the Communion Service, the best of all comments on the Scriptures appertaining to this mystery. And this is the preparation which will prove, with God's grace, the surest preventive of, or antidote against, the freezing poison, the lethargizing hemlock of the doctrine of the Sacramentaries, according to whom the Eucharist is a mere practical metaphor, in which things are employed instead of articulated sounds for the exclusive purpose of recalling to our minds the historical fact of our

Lord's crucifixion; in short (the profaneness is with them, not with me), just the same as when Protestants drink a glass of wine to the glorious memory of William III. ! True it is that the remembrance is one end of the Sacrament; but it is, "*Do this in remembrance of Me*"—of all that Christ was and is, hath done and is still doing for fallen mankind, and, of course, of His crucifixion inclusively, but not of His crucifixion alone. December 14, 1827.'*

Coleridge was, in fact, instrumental in bringing about in the minds of many thinking men a similar change to that which had occurred in his own mind. He was brought up in Unitarian principles, which he eventually rejected. He was feeling his way towards Catholic truth, a great deal of which he apprehended; and his evidence in its favour is the more satisfactory, inasmuch as he never states an opinion or doctrine without fully demonstrating its reasonableness. It is significant that his 'Aids to Reflection' consist very largely of selected passages from the saintly Archbishop Leighton, with Coleridge's comments and amplifications. I believe this celebrated book is sometimes regarded as the foundation of what is known as the Broad Church theology. This school arose during the course of the Oxford Movement. It was partly the result of a reaction against its extreme tendencies, partly the combination of various forces, not altogether unfriendly to it, but all, whether opposing the mediævalism of the movement or not, distinctly breaking away from the Protestantism hitherto dominant. Both the Catholic and the Broad Church schools were greatly indebted to Coleridge. Dean Church thus refers to him: 'In England another recluse (the first was Mr. Alexander Knox) of splendid genius and wayward humour had dealt in his own way, with far-reaching insight, with vast reading, and often with impressive eloquence, with the same subject (the Christian Church); and his profound sympathy and faith had been shared and reflected by a great poet. What Coleridge and Wordsworth had put in the forefront of their

* 'Confessions of an Inquiring Spirit.'

speculations and poetry, as the object of their profoundest interest and of their highest hopes for mankind, might, of course, fail to appear in the same light to others; but it could not fail, in those days at least, to attract attention, as a matter of grave and well-founded importance. Coleridge's theories of the Church were his own, and were very wide of theories recognised by any of those who had to deal practically with the question, and who were influenced in one way or another by the traditional doctrines of theologians. But Coleridge had lifted the subject to a very high level. He had taken the simple but all-important step of viewing the Church in its spiritual character as first and foremost, and above all things essentially a religious society of Divine institution, not dependent on the creation or will of man, or on the privileges and honours which man might think fit to assign to it; and he had undoubtedly familiarized the minds of many with this way of regarding it, however imperfect, or cloudy, or unpractical they might find the development of his ideas and his deductions from them.'*

However much these (*i.e.*, the Catholic and Broad) schools differed from each other (and they had much more in common than a superficial observer might suppose, as has since been proved by their partial coalescence), they differed still more from the current religionism. There was at least that sort of sympathy between them which must always arise between two independent sets of thinkers and writers, both in a minority, but both numbering some of the brightest intellects of the day in their ranks.

It is noticeable that Coleridge and his brother-in-law, Southey, were both ardent admirers of Bishop Jeremy Taylor. There is a beautiful passage in Southey's 'Thálaba,' which is nothing more than a transcription from one of Taylor's sermons slightly altered into blank verse.†

Coleridge again and again breaks out into quotation

* 'Oxford Movement,' ch. viii.
† It was in the course of a lecture on Bishop Taylor that I called

from this master of poetic prose. The fascination which Bishop Taylor exercised over both these men was perhaps chiefly that of one poet on another. His boundless wealth of illustration, whether from the world of nature or from the poets of classical antiquity, the freedom and luxuriance of his language, so different from the stereotyped manner of the evangelical divines, was naturally appreciated by such men as the Lake writers. But there was a deeper ground of affinity. Taylor represented a school which was a reaction against the narrow Protestantism and puritanism of his day. This accounts for the liberality and generosity which run through his works. His 'Liberty of Prophesying' is perhaps the most remarkable book of its time, so vastly ahead is it of temporary and local prejudice ; in fact,

---

attention to his influence on the Lake writers. The particular verse in 'Thálaba' is the 16th of Book VIII. :

'. . . . behold this vine,
I found it a wild tree, whose wanton strength
    Had swoln into irregular twigs
    And bold excrescences,
And spent itself in leaves and little rings,
So in the flourish of its outwardness
    Wasting the sap and strength
That should have given forth fruit ;
    But when I prun'd the tree,
Then it grew temperate in its vain expense
Of useless leaves, and knotted, as thou seest,
Into these full, clear clusters, to repay
    The hand that wisely wounded it.'

The original passage is as follows : 'For so have I known a luxuriant vine swell into irregular twigs and bold excrescences, and spend itself in leaves and little rings, and afford but trifling clusters to the wine-press, and a faint return to his heart which longed to be refreshed with a full vintage ; but when the lord of the vine had caused the dressers to cut the wilder plant and made it bleed, it grew temperate in its vain expense of useless leaves, and knotted into fair and juicy branches, and made accounts of that loss of blood by the return of fruit.'

Southey truly says that he has altered the unimprovable language of the original as little as possible.

as has been sarcastically observed, it was in advance of the writer himself in the days of his prosperity. Taylor, in short, was one of those grand souls who belong to no school or party; he was what we should call a Catholic in the largest sense of the expression. Now, Robert Leighton, who I have shown was Coleridge's model in the 'Aids,' was very similarly constituted. He was worried by the Presbyterians for his personal friendship with Romanists, while he was too keenly alive to the errors of their Church to be reckoned on their side theologically. This position of the *Via Media* held by Taylor and held by Leighton, was also attained by Coleridge and Southey.

While Coleridge was writing on the side of truth, as he conceived it, in the language of 'philosophic meditation,' Southey was busy on the same side as an essayist and historian, in addition to what he produced in verse. His 'Thálaba,' a poem, curiously enough, of which Dr. Newman was one of the few admirers, appeared in 1801, and was followed by several other poetical works. But, like Scott, it is by his *prose* that Southey is best known, and by which he has chiefly influenced his generation. From 1808 to 1838 he wrote over ninety articles for the *Quarterly Review*. His mind, the result of his vast reading in various directions, was eclectic, in the sense that it was a curious mixture of English, French, and German philosophies — Goethe, Rousseau, and Gibbon had each a pretty good share in the formation of his views—while in religious matters, though not free from the taint of Unitarianism, his weight has been chiefly on the side of the Church. The wide and independent field of his secular reading, while preventing him from being what is called *orthodox* on all points of Church doctrine, was a guarantee of his Catholicity in the broader sense of the term. His one distinct ecclesiastical effort was his 'Book of the Church,' published in 1824, which has done good service historically, in anticipation of doctrinal works on the same subject since put forth by the Oxford writers.

In a word, he broke away from the traditional *low* view of the Church, and prepared his readers for higher and more Catholic views of it than he himself actually stated.

In the article in the *British Critic* already referred to (see note on p. 29), Cardinal Newman bears eloquent witness to the good work of the writers I have mentioned. I quote the passage as repeated in the 'Apologia': 'After thus stating the phenomenon of the time, as it presented itself to those who did not sympathize with it, the article proceeds to account for it; and this it does by considering it as a reaction from the dry and superficial character of the religious teaching and the literature of the last generation or century, and as a result of the need which was felt both by the hearts and the intellects of the nation for a deeper philosophy, and as the evidence and as the partial fulfilment of that need, to which even the chief authors of the then generation had borne witness. First, I mentioned the literary influence of Walter Scott, who turned men's minds in the direction of the Middle Ages. "The general need," I said, "of something deeper and more attractive than what had offered itself elsewhere may be considered to have led to his popularity; and by means of his popularity he reacted on his readers, stimulating their mental thirst, feeding their hopes, setting before them visions which, when once seen, are not easily forgotten, and silently indoctrinating them with nobler ideas, which might afterwards be appealed to as first principles." Then I spoke of Coleridge thus: "While history in prose and verse was thus made the instrument of Church feelings and opinions, a philosophical basis for the same was laid in England by a very original thinker, who, while he indulged a liberty of speculation which no Christian can tolerate, and advocated conclusions which were often heathen rather than Christian, yet, after all, installed a higher philosophy into inquiring minds than they had hitherto been accustomed to accept. In this way he made trial of his age, and succeeded in interesting its genius in the cause of Catholic truth." Then come Southey and Wordsworth, "two living poets, one of whom in the department of fantastic fiction, the other in that of philosophic meditation, have addressed themselves to the same high principles and feelings, and carried forward their readers in the same direction."[*]

There is one more name about which I must say something as participating in the intellectual movements of the day, and whose influence, I think, we may venture to throw into the Catholic scale. I refer to Thomas de Quincey, the English opium-eater. Master of language as he was, he only wrote *two books*—one a little work on political economy, the other a German romance called 'Klosterheim.' These two books will show the extent of his genius. He wrote on an immense variety of subjects between them, but all his other writings came out as magazine articles. The reason, probably, was that, like his friend Coleridge, he lacked the steady application which the manufacture of books requires; or possibly that the examination of minute details in which his genius delighted, and which was constantly leading him off the main lines of his subject, would prevent his undertaking what he could scarcely have done in an ordinary lifetime.

This probably applies to both writers. If I am not mistaken, both projected certain large works which were never executed. Had they been more active, or more capable of concentration and condensation, we might have had some very instructive Church history from them. De Quincey abounds in passages showing that he was not fettered by Protestant prejudice. Thus, in commenting on Newman's work on 'Development':

'Without meaning to undertake a defence of Mr. Newman (whose book I am as yet too slenderly acquainted with), may I be allowed at this point to intercept a fallacious view of that doctrine, as though essentially it

[*] 'Apologia,' ch. iii.

proclaimed some imperfection in Christianity? The imperfection is in us, the Christians, not in Christianity. . . . In the course of a day or a year the sun passes through a wide variety of positions, aspects, and corresponding powers in relation to ourselves. Daily and annually he is *developed* to us—he runs a cycle of development. Yet, after all, this practical result does not argue any change or imperfection, growth or decay, in the sun. This great orb is stationary as regards his place, and unchanging as regards his power. It is the subjective change in ourselves that projects itself into this endless succession of *apparent* changes in the object. Not otherwise on the scheme of religious development,' etc.*

His remarks on casuistry, again, are very suggestive:

'Our fashionable moral practitioner for this generation, Dr. Paley, who prescribes for the consciences of both universities, and, indeed, of most respectable householders, has introduced a good deal of casuistry into his work, though not under that name. In England there is an aversion to the real name, founded partly on this,—that casuistry has been most cultivated by Roman Catholic divines, and too much with a view to an indulgent and dispensing morality, and partly on the excessive subdivision and hair-splitting of cases, which tends to the infinite injury of morals, by perplexing and tampering with the conscience, and by presuming morality to be above the powers of any but the subtlest minds. All this, however, is but the abuse of casuistry; and without casuistry of some sort or other no practical decision could be made in the accidents of daily life,' etc.†

This vein of thought reappears elsewhere in De Quincey, notably in his 'Essay on Casuistry.'

I have tried to show that there has been a chain of writers from the days of the Reformation to the opening

* 'Essay on Protestantism.'
† Note to Letter II. to a young man.

of the present century by whom the Catholic theology was kept alive within the Church of England; that the Oxford men were not stating new doctrines so much as recurring to the hereditary teaching; that when they arose men's minds were stirred in various directions; that various religious movements were in embryo, and that the so-called Oxford Movement was but one of many manifestations of an intellectual activity then permeating educated society. And consequently, in addition to the older writers to whom the Tractarians were able to appeal, they had their immediate precursors and contemporaries, who (involuntarily, perhaps, but still most effectually) prepared the public mind for the reception of the truths they had to deliver. To put it in Cardinal Newman's own words: 'Those doctrines were in the air—the movement in which they were taking part was the birth of a crisis rather than of a place.'* Or in the words of Dean Church: 'The time was ripe for great collisions of principles and aims; for the decomposition of elements which had been hitherto united; for sifting them out of their old combinations, and regrouping them according to their more natural affinities. It was a time for the formation and development of unexpected novelties in teaching and practical effort. There was a great historic Church party imperfectly conscious of its position and responsibilities; there was an active but declining pietistic school resting on a feeble intellectual basis and narrow and meagre interpretations of Scripture, and strong only in its circle of philanthropic work; there was, confronting both, a rising body of inquisitive and, in some ways, menacing thought. To men deeply interested in religion the ground seemed confused and treacherous. There was room, and there was a call, for new effort; but to find the resources for it, it seemed necessary to cut down deep below the level of what even good men accepted as the adequate expression of Christianity, and its fit applica-

* 'Apologia.'

tion to the conditions of the nineteenth century.'* Or, again, in the words of Dean Burgon: 'To read of the great Church Revival of 1833 as it presents itself to the imagination of certain writers, one would suppose that, in their account, the publication of the earliest of the "Tracts for the Times" had the magical effect of kindling into glory the dead embers of an all but extinct Church. The plain truth is, that the smouldering materials for the cheerful blaze which followed the efforts made in 1832-3-4 had been accumulating unobserved for many years—had been the residuum of the altar-fires of a long succession of holy and earnest men. . . . As at another famous occasion of national apostasy, God was found to have "reserved to Himself seven thousand" who had retained their hold on Catholic truth amid every discouragement. . . . Church feeling was *evoked*, not *created*, by the movement of 1833.'†

This last quotation is followed by a list of about forty men to whom the remark applied, not one of whom I have mentioned, because I have rather sought to trace the origin of the movement through courses not usually supposed to have any connexion with it, than through such more obvious channels as the Dean refers to.

* 'Oxford Movement,' ch. i.
† Biographical sketch of Hugh James Rose.

LECTURE III.

THE OXFORD MOVEMENT: ITS LEADERS AND SUPPORTERS.

AFTER the death of John Keble, Cardinal Newman was asked to write something about the man and his works. He respectfully declined on the ground of their old acquaintance, which made criticism impossible, as it included so much that could not be publicly discussed without violating the sacred laws of friendship. Some such feeling as this must necessarily be present to any thoughtful person when contemplating the lives of great men departed, especially men of marked sanctity of character whose works have made them in a sense his personal friends. And the reluctance to speak freely will naturally be greater when those men belong to our own times, when the details of their lives are more or less familiar to everybody, and when numberless recollections will be stirred in the minds of one's hearers, whether friendly or adverse to the characters concerned.

It is with a strong feeling of hesitation, therefore, not to say of reverential regard, that I venture to say anything about those great men who are regarded as the prime movers in the Catholic revival. But our subject requires me to say something, and the stage at which we have arrived makes it necessary that I should say it at once.

To recur to a remark which I have previously let fall. We must all have been struck by the fact that great movements usually originate with a single person, who possibly gives them a name, or, at all events, to whose individual energy they can be traced. The peculiarity of the Oxford Movement is that it seems rather to have been the birth of the times, to have been due to some spirit stirring the air and affecting a number of people simultaneously, than to have arisen in any single mind whom alone we can hold responsible for it. There can be no doubt whatever that Newman was the master-mind throughout, though he modestly disclaims the position of a leader, and the public instinct was probably correct in conferring the name of *Newmanites* on the party as pointing to the great personality which was its inspiring genius. But that there really was some doubt about the leadership, or that different people were inclined to place it elsewhere according to their notions of personal influence, or that the movement assumed a different character from time to time as one or other of its agents became more prominent, is evidenced by the fact that the name was repeatedly changed.

The Rev. T. Mozley says that 'had Keble remained quite as he was for two or three years more, and others been content to preach and to talk, half Oxford and a great part of England would have been called *Kebleans* to this day most probably.' Dr. Pusey's name was ultimately adopted as implying the most permanent and solid, though not the most brilliant, influence. But, as Dean Church suggests, the reason was probably that it contained a touch of the comic when supplemented by the usual affix.

An old clerical friend of mine used to tell a story about a visitor to a country church where such mild innovations as a surpliced choir and preaching in a surplice had been introduced. 'Pray,' said the stranger to the verger, 'are there *many* Puseyites about in this neighbourhood?' 'Well, sir,' replied the verger, 'there still be a few left, but there's not so many as there used to be.' 'Oh, indeed; I am very glad to hear it. And, pray, how do you account for the falling off?' 'Why, the fact is, sir, *we takes their eggs in the spring.*' The rustic attendant thought that *peewits* were referred to.

As a matter of fact, the name in general use was first Newmanites, then Puseyites, both names being, as usual, bestowed by outsiders, and however honourable they may have since become (indeed, they have become so honourable that they have been discontinued), they originally conveyed, and were intended to convey, a certain amount of ridicule.

The meeting of friends and the ventilation of subjects, which eventually found expression in the 'Tracts for the Times,' dates back to the year 1829, when Newman and certain fellows and undergraduates of the University began to meet twice a week for the study of Scripture. As T. Mozley points out, there was a curious resemblance between these meetings and those of Wesley and his friends exactly a hundred years before. It seems that biblical scholarship was in a very low state at the University in those days, and though the New Testament was studied, the exercises chiefly consisted of construing and examining some points of grammatical scholarship. Those who wished to derive any special religious benefit from the Bible had to do so from their private reading or from conversation at such gatherings as Newman and his friends arranged.

The first book chosen for consideration was the Revelation of St. John the Divine, for the simple reason that prophecy was then a favourite subject, and students were much exercised in attempts at the identification of Antichrist. The choice apparently lay between Mohammed, Napoleon Buonaparte, the Pope, and the Church of Rome. The days had gone by when the first could seriously be considered, and the downfall of the second at Waterloo decided the question against the unfortunate Papacy. At least, if that were *not*, the difficulty was to discover who (or what) *was* Antichrist.

The resemblance of Rome to the supposed characteristics was sufficiently close in the Protestant apprehension, but people of a Catholic disposition naturally argued that to be like Antichrist implied a resemblance to Christ Himself.

An ingenious compromise presented itself by transferring the identity from the Church of Rome to the pagan city, over which the old spirit of heathenism might still be supposed to hover. Questions of doctrinal difference between England and Rome were then quite in abeyance, possibly because they had been settled so satisfactorily long ago that it was thought waste of time to reopen them. Anyhow, there was a general ignorance on such subjects, and they were not taught officially at the University or from the pulpit. We can easily understand that from this very circumstance points of Roman controversy would naturally be raised at these private meetings which could not be discussed elsewhere. This would also be the inevitable tendency of the prophetic matter; and the particular circumstances of the Church of England, referred to in our first lecture, would stimulate inquiry in the same direction. Anyhow, such questions were raised and discussed, and the whole subject of the relations of England to Rome was reopened, with the inevitable result of a contrast between the two Churches, and an examination of the weak points of the former. Here subjects were ventilated which afterwards came before the public, and minds were stirred to think who afterwards wrote so ably about them.

It may be interesting to notice, in passing, the relations between Newman and his college pupils when he was one of the tutors of Oriel. He was on much closer terms of friendship with them than usually subsisted in Oxford between tutors and pupils. He did more for them, and expected more from them, than was enough to satisfy the average teacher. And his influence was of course immense, as must always be the case where a man of superior intellect and scholarship unbends to those beneath him officially. This is perhaps the proper place to mention that in tracing the career of this great man we shall find it divides itself into four very natural stages. He was first influential as a tutor, then as a parish priest, then as a preacher, and lastly as a writer, each of which meant an extension of influence beyond that which preceded it.

The spirit which was at work quietly at Oxford, and in various minds elsewhere, was evoked into public activity several years later by an event which has given a date to the revival. 'On July 14, 1833,' Cardinal Newman tells us in his 'Apologia,' 'Mr. Keble preached the assize sermon in the University pulpit. It was published under the title of "National Apostasy." I have ever considered and kept the day as the start of the religious movement of 1833.'

In a letter to his father's old friend, Mr. Richards, Keble refers to the immediate result of his sermon as follows :

'Some of my friends at Oxford—persons worthy of much confidence—are wishing for a kind of association to circulate right notions on the Apostolical Succession, and also for the defence of the Prayer-Book against any sort of profane innovation, which seems too likely to be attempted. Might we hope for your countenance and support if such a thing should be set on foot? Isaac Williams, I think, has been written to, and can give you all particulars about it. I cannot help hoping that there is still a good deal of cordial Church feeling about the country, which it is very desirable to encourage in a quiet way, and to get people to dwell on it a little more.'

If man is a microcosm, I suppose we may fairly compare a great public movement with what sometimes happens in the life of an individual. Circumstances have led a man's thoughts in a particular direction—say to be uneasy about his own spiritual state, or about the condition of his fellow-men. He goes on thinking about the matter, perhaps discussing it with anyone who will give him a hearing, till it takes such hold of his mind as to exclude every other subject. In common parlance, he goes mad upon it. Perhaps the expression is true, or it may be merely a way of putting that excessive interest and enthusiasm which ordinary men cannot account for on any other hypothesis. While the man is in this condition something happens to him. He has been a great sinner; he hears a striking sermon, is converted, and founds a new religious order. He hears a powerful political speech, and is converted in another sense into a patriot. If his genius is of a literary turn, his lonely imaginings are stirred into activity by some literary masterpiece. His latent talent is brought out, and he writes a famous book.

In every such case thought precedes action, and the latter is evoked by a collision of the subjective with the objective. The man *does* something which leaves a mark on society, gets him a great name, or perhaps the honour of martyrdom. This is often the history of great public benefactors, of great religious teachers, of great writers. And when a number of people are simultaneously stirred by the same impulse, however cold and phlegmatic they may be in their own nature, they become heated and inflamed by mutual contact. The result will depend on the character of the persons concerned. It may be a deadly fanaticism, such as is exhibited in great rebellions, or a healthy enthusiasm for the moral or religious benefit of society. In one case we may have such a movement as the French Revolution; in the other such a philanthropic movement as that for the abolition of slavery, or a religious revival like that we are considering.

Mr. Keble's sermon was the immediate occasion for that systematic course of action which resulted in the 'Tracts for the Times.' It was, as it were, the trumpet which called men together for united and concentrated effort, who had hitherto been thinking and acting separately. The first practical step was a small meeting of friends, held at the parsonage of Mr. Hugh James Rose, at Hadleigh, in

Suffolk, during the same month (July) in which the sermon was preached. At this gathering the thoughts and anxieties which had filled the minds of a number of earnest Churchmen, and had brought them into communication with one another, came to a head, and issued in a decision to act in concert.

It is a striking fact that Mr. Rose, whose name is not now popularly associated with the revival, was at that initial stage its presiding genius, and his high character and literary distinction made him the most suitable person to call together such a meeting and to control its deliberations. The fourth volume of Newman's 'Parochial Sermons' bears the following beautiful dedication: 'To the Rev. Hugh James Rose, B.D., Principal of King's College, London, and domestic Chaplain to the Archbishop of Canterbury, who when hearts were failing bade us stir up the gift that was in us, and betake ourselves to our true Mother.'

Mr. Rose's allies were Mr. William Palmer, Mr. A. Perceval, Mr. Froude, Mr. Keble, and Mr. Newman, the first four of whom only were actually present, while the last two acted by correspondence. All these men were in complete agreement on the main subject, but, as we should expect from men of their marked personality and individual habits of thought, they otherwise differed considerably.

For an account of Mr. Rose I cannot do better than quote the words of Dean Church: 'Mr. Rose was a man whose name and whose influence, as his friends thought, have been overshadowed and overlooked in the popular view of the Church Revival. It owed to him, they held, not only its first impulse, but all that was best and most hopeful in it, and when it lost him, it lost its wisest and ablest guide and inspirer. It is certainly true that when that Revival began he was much more distinguished and important than any of the other persons interested in it. As far as could be seen at the time, he was the most accomplished divine and teacher in the English Church. He was a really learned man. He had the intellect and energy and literary skill to use his learning. He was a man of singularly elevated and religious character; he had something of the eye and temper of a statesman, and he had already a high position. He was profoundly loyal to the Church, and keenly interested in whatever affected its condition and its fortunes. As early as 1825 he had in some lectures at Cambridge called the attention of English Churchmen to the state of religious thought and speculation in Germany, and to the mischiefs likely to react on English theology from the rationalizing temper and methods which had supplanted the old Lutheran teaching; and this had led to a sharp controversy with Mr. Pusey, as he was then, who thought that Mr. Rose had both exaggerated the fact itself, and had not adequately given the historical account of it. He had the prudence, but not the backwardness, of a man of large knowledge and considerable experience of the world. More alive to difficulties and dangers than his younger associates, he showed his courage and his unselfish earnestness in his frank sympathy with them, daring and outspoken as they were, and in his willingness to share with them the risks of an undertaking of which no one knew better than he what were likely to be the difficulties. He certainly was a person who might be expected to have a chief part in directing anything with which he was connected. His countenance and his indirect influence were very important elements, both in the stirring of thought which led to the Hadleigh resolutions, and in giving its form to what was then decided upon. But his action in the movement was impeded by his failure in health and cut short by his early death, January, 1839.'*

Dean Burgon speaks of him as follows: 'It will become more and more apparent as we proceed that if *to any one man* is to be assigned the honour of having originated the great Catholic Revival of our times, *that* man was Hugh

* 'Oxford Movement.'—The correct date of his death was December 22, 1838.

James Rose. For my own part, I am inclined to think that it fares with such movements as it fares with rivers. Their true source, their actual fountain-head, is remote, is insignificant. A confluence of brooks produces in time a stream, into which many tributaries discharge themselves; the channel deepens, widens, receives somewhere a considerable accession of waters, and now, behold, it has become a mighty river! ... So was it with the great Catholic Revival of which we speak. But it remains true, for all that, that amid the forms which crowd around us, and the voices which make themselves heard above the " hurly-burly," when the history of a great work is to be deliberately committed to writing, *one* authoritative voice, *one* commanding figure becomes conspicuous beyond the rest; and posterity will recognise the fact that it was Hugh James Rose who was the true moving cause of that stirring of the waters which made an indelible impress on the Church of England between fifty and sixty years ago, and which it is customary to date from the autumn of 1833. It was he who, so early as the year 1822, had pointed out to the clergy *Internal Union* as " the best safeguard against the dangers of the Church." In 1825, as we have seen, from the University pulpit at Cambridge, he had directed attention to the state of German Protestantism—a spectacle of warning to the Church of England. But it was by his soul-stirring discourses on the commission of the clergy, preached before the same University in 1826, that he chiefly recalled men's attention to those great Church principles which had all but universally fallen into neglect, if not oblivion. ... Now, therefore, when the sky grew darkest and most threatening (1829-1831), and the muttering thunder was filling men's souls with a terrible anticipation of the coming storm, all eyes were instinctively turned to *him* as the fittest to lead and to guide. The bishops should have taken the initiative, and put themselves at the head of the movement; but not one of them stirred, and no one dared approach them. The diocesan organization to which the genius of Samuel Wilberforce, Bishop of Oxford, some twenty years later, imparted such efficient flexibility, as yet existed only in theory. Let it in fairness be confessed that the traditional cumbrous exclusiveness of their exalted station, not to say the suspicions under which they laboured as a body, disqualified our then bishops from the kind of action which at the close of the first quarter of the present century had become a necessity. Thus it happened that a standard-bearer had to be sought for elsewhere; and, as we have said, the man on whom Churchmen fixed their hopes was Hugh James Rose.'*

Dean Church writes as follows of Mr. William Palmer, of Worcester College: 'He had been educated at Trinity College, Dublin, but he had transferred his home to Oxford, both in the University and in the city. He was a man of exact and scholastic mind, well equipped at all points in controversial theology, strong in clear theories and precise definitions, familiar with objections current in the schools and with the answers to them, and well versed in all the questions, arguments, and authorities belonging to the great debate with Rome. He had definite and well-arranged ideas about the nature and office of the Church; and, from his study of the Roman controversy, he had at command the distinctions necessary to discriminate between things which popular views confused, and to protect the doctrines characteristic of the Church from being identified with Romanism. Especially he had given great attention to the public devotional language and forms of the Church, and had produced by far the best book in the English language on the history and significance of the offices of the English Church—the "Origines Liturgicæ," published at the University Press in 1832. It was a book to give a man authority with divines and scholars; and among those with whom at this time he acted no one had so compact and defensible a

* 'Lives of Twelve Good Men.'

theory, even if it was somewhat rigid and technical, of the peculiar constitution of the English Church as Mr. Palmer. With the deepest belief in his theory, he saw great dangers threatening, partly from general ignorance and looseness of thought, partly from antagonistic ideas and principles only too distinct and too popular; and he threw all his learning and zeal on the side of those who, like himself, were alive to those dangers, and were prepared for a great effort to counteract them.'*

As regards Mr. A. Perceval, the Rev. T. Mozley describes his connection with the movement as casual; he says:

'Several writers, in particular Mr. Perceval, conceived a most extraordinary idea of the "Hadleigh Conference," as if it were at once a great beginning and a great finality. They who heard of it as one of the many incidents of the day can only be surprised that any man of sense should think it possible Newman, or even Froude, should be comprised and shut up by a few strokes of the pen, and henceforth warranted to keep pace with so very casual an acquaintance as Mr. Perceval.'†

On the other hand fairness compels us to reckon Mr. Perceval among the chief actors in the early stages of the movement, in furtherance of which he had done good service, even before the meeting at Hadleigh, by the publication of a work which he regarded as the *first* of the 'Tracts for the Times.' It was a small catechism called the 'Churchman's Manual,' intended as a sort of supplement to the Church Catechism for giving instruction about the Church and its ministers, which was certainly omitted from the official work. Mr. Rose, Mr. Palmer, and Mr. Froude were also instrumental in its compilation, *i.e.*, in the way of suggestion and revision, and it was submitted to a great many theological experts before publication, with the view of such careful construction as should secure for it the *imprimatur* of the Bench of Bishops. This, however, was

* 'Oxford Movement.' † 'Reminiscences.'

refused, as, although no objection was raised to the contents of the book, it was not thought expedient to give it official sanction. In one sense this little Catechism *was* the first of the Tracts, or, rather, their precursor; but it does not belong to the series, and has been completely overshadowed by the more weighty publications of greater writers.

We now come to Richard Hurrell Froude, whom Mozley is inclined to place on a level with Newman in the speculative question (as he calls it) as to who was the master spirit of the movement.

'Froude was a man,' he says, 'such as there are now and then, of whom it is impossible for those that have known him to speak without exceeding the bounds of common admiration and affection. He was elder brother of William, the distinguished engineer, who died lately, after rendering, and while still rendering, most important services to the Admiralty, and of Anthony, the well-known historian, the sons of Archdeacon Froude, a scholar and no mean artist. Richard came to Oriel from Eton, a school which does not make every boy a scholar, if it even tries to do so, but which somehow implants in every nature a generous ambition of one kind or other. As an undergraduate he waged a ruthless war against sophistry and loud talk, and he gibbeted one or two victims, labelling their sophisms with their names. Elected to a Fellowship, and now the companion of Newman and Pusey, not to speak of elders and juniors, he had to wield his weapons more reverentially and warily. But he had no wish to do otherwise.

'His figure and manner were such as to command the confidence and affection of those about him. Tall, erect, very thin, never resting or sparing himself, investigating and explaining with unwearied energy, incisive in his language, and with a certain fiery force of look and tone, he seemed a sort of angelic presence to weaker natures. He slashed at the shams, phrases, and disguises in which the lazy or the pretentious veil their real ignorance or folly. His features readily expressed every varying mood of playfulness, sadness, and awe. There were those about him who would rather writhe under his most cutting sarcasms than miss their part in the workings of his sympathy and genius. Froude was a Tory, of that transcendental idea of the English gentleman which forms the basis of Toryism. He was a High Churchman of the uncompromising school, very early taking part with Anselm, Becket, Laud, and the Nonjurors. Woe to anyone who dropped in his hearing such phrases as the "dark ages," "superstition," "bigotry," "right of private judgment," "enlightenment," "march of mind" or "progress." When a strong man of science fell back on "law," or a "subtle medium," or any other device for making matter its own lord and master, it was as if a fox had broken cover; there ensued a chase and no mercy. Luxury, show, and even comfort he despised and denounced.'*

In the original draft of this lecture and in its actual delivery I had inserted a brief sketch of the other members of the Hadleigh conference—Keble and Newman, as well as of Dr. Pusey and the other leading contributors to the 'Tracts for the Times.' With the exception of a few personal recollections, the information then given is too well known to need a public repetition, and I therefore omit it, supposing that most people interested in the subject have read Coleridge's or Lock's 'Life of Keble,' Cardinal Newman's 'Apologia' (in which he is practically his own biographer), and the volumes that have appeared of Canon Liddon's *magnum opus* on Dr. Pusey. It may be useful, however, to say a few words about the Tracts themselves, which obtained the name of *Tractarians* to their authors and those sharing their opinions. The first three bear the

---

* 'Reminiscences.' — Those who have time should supplement the above with the graphic recollections of Froude (communicated by Lord Blachford) in the third chapter of Dean Church's 'Oxford Movement.'

date of September 9, 1833; the last was published on February 27, 1841, and, as shall shortly be explained, brought the series to an abrupt termination. Their object was to call attention to such doctrines as the apostolic succession, the real (though spiritual) presence of Christ in the Eucharist, baptismal regeneration, the true nature of the Christian Church, its authority, constitution, doctrines, and ritual. These doctrines were practically ignored at the time, and it was to this circumstance that the writers attributed the state of degradation into which the Church of England had fallen. It was in their revival, therefore, that they placed their hopes of its restoration to life and energy. But the intention of the writers cannot better be stated than in their own words, prefixed in the shape of an 'advertisement' to the first forty-six Tracts, when they were collected into a volume towards the end of the year 1834:

'The following tracts were published with the object of contributing something towards the practical revival of doctrines which, although held by the great divines of our Church, at present have become obsolete with the majority of her members, and are withdrawn from public view even by the more learned and orthodox few who still adhere to them. The apostolic succession, the Holy Catholic Church, were principles of action in the minds of our predecessors of the seventeenth century; but in proportion as the maintenance of the Church has been secured by law, her ministers have been under the temptation of leaning on an arm of flesh instead of her own Divinely-provided discipline, a temptation increased by political events and arrangements which need not here be more than alluded to.'

Dr. Pusey had previously given a single Tract (No. 18) to the series, but it was not till about this time that he became connected with them as an active contributor. His accession, as Dr. Newman states, was a great gain, both from the weight of his personal character and influence, and from the change which his co-operation induced in the character of the papers, which from brief leaflets were expanded into treatises of permanent theological value.

'Dr. Pusey was, to use the common expression, a host in himself; he was able to give a name, a form, and a personality to what was without him a sort of mob. . . . Such was the benefit which he conferred on the movement externally; nor were the internal advantages at all inferior to it. He was a man of large designs; he had a hopeful, sanguine mind; he had no fear of others; he was haunted by no intellectual perplexities. . . . Dr. Pusey's influence was felt at once. He saw that there ought to be more sobriety, more gravity, more careful pains, more sense of responsibility in the Tracts and in the whole movement. It was through him that the character of the Tracts was changed. When he gave to us his 'Tract on Fasting' he put his initials to it. In 1835 he published his elaborate 'Treatise on Baptism,' which was followed by other Tracts from different authors, if not of equal learning, yet of equal power and appositeness.'*

The excitement caused by these papers is scarcely intelligible to us at the present day, now that the doctrines contended for are so generally held; but they appeared amid such profound ignorance, and such dense incapacity to distinguish between Roman and Catholic, that people were frightened out of their wits at what they thought was unmitigated Popery. The Tracts which created the greatest alarm were those (Nos. 80 and 87) by Isaac Williams, on 'Reserve in Communicating Religious Knowledge,' and the last of the series (decidedly not the least), No. 90, by John Henry Newman.

Both these writers ran directly counter to the popular religious notions of the day—the first in pointing out certain dangers in that unreserved circulation of Scripture which was thought the chief bulwark of Protestantism, and in popularizing (or vulgarizing) such a sacred doctrine as that

* 'Apologia.'

of the Atonement; the second in appearing to sanction certain Romish doctrines, which the Articles had hitherto been understood to condemn.

As regards religious knowledge, that there *are* dangers in too great freedom in both the points I have mentioned will generally be granted. We have an illustration in modern elementary education, *i.e.*, in conveying a knowledge of the Bible without a corresponding training of character. The words of Tract LXXX. are as appropriate as if they had just been written for a School Board controversy:

'With regard to national schools, I would be careful not to say anything that might appear to depreciate the value of religious knowledge, but to say that such knowledge is a treasure of so transcendent a nature, that it must be handled with sacred care, is not to depreciate, but to exalt its value. As our Lord led persons gradually to the knowledge of the truth by quiet teaching, by leading them to observe His works, by drawing out their self-denial and engaging their confidence, so, in obedience to His command "to make *disciples* of all nations," the system of the Church is that of parental and pastoral training, and building up by practical instruction, such as catechizing and the use of a constant devotional form. These not having been sufficiently carried on has given rise to two effects: the one is an undue preponderance given to preaching, in order to supply the want, as if it were powerfully to bring to the heart that knowledge which has not been received into the character by gradual inculcation and discipline; the other effect has been the system of large national schools, the object of which is contrary to the spirit of the Church, to impart sacred knowledge without any of this training as coinciding with it, except in a very limited way, and to inculcate knowledge without adequately instilling a sense of its practical importance.'

And as regards the unreserved communication of sacred *doctrines*, every sensible Churchman must be alive to its dangers, with the spectacle before him of certain modern sects, who in their anxiety to bring home the Gospel (as it is called, which is practically limited to the Atonement) to the minds of uneducated people, have adopted a slang vocabulary and vulgar illustrations for the purpose, to the detriment of that spirit of *reverence* which the Church system tends to secure.

But the strong position of the writer is attested by a critic of an opposite school, who, amidst a good deal of blame, acknowledges the general force of the Tract as follows: 'These arguments, which are scattered over the Tracts without much regard to order, are drawn from a variety of sources. Philosophy and natural instinct, Scripture and tradition, are all made to combine in enforcing the duty of reserve for which the writer pleads. And he is able to show, apparently to his own perfect satisfaction, that we are contradicting the best established principles of mental philosophy, resisting the right impulses of the nature which God has bestowed upon us, going against the genius and spirit of all Divine teaching, whether in providence or revelation, but more especially rejecting the lesson which is taught us by the example of the blessed Lord Himself, and finally opposing the principles of the Catholic Church, when we publish this great mystery to men of unholy lives.'*

As regards Tract XC., that there was an error of judgment in the time of its issue, and the mode in which the subject was treated, may be conceded—in fact, I believe, has practically been conceded by the author himself. But that there was a need for some such elucidation of the Articles has been made clear by the various works on them which have since appeared, notably the celebrated work of Dr. Harold Browne, which have also made it clear that the Articles do admit of the Catholic interpretation put upon them by Dr. Newman in his Tract. His own opinion may

* Charge of Bishop O'Brien of Ossory to his clergy, published in 1843.

be gathered from the letter he addressed in 1841 to Canon Jelf as an *Apologia* for what he had written :

'In truth there is at this moment a great progress of the religious mind of our Church to something deeper and truer than satisfied the last century. I always have contended, and will contend, that it is not satisfactorily accounted for by any particular movement of individuals on a particular spot. The poets and philosophers of the age have borne witness to it many years. Those great names in our literature—Sir Walter Scott, Mr. Wordsworth, Mr. Coleridge—though in different ways and with essential differences one from another, and perhaps from any Church system, still all bear witness to it. Mr. Alexander Knox in Ireland bears a most surprising witness to it. The system of Mr. Irving is another witness to it. The age is moving towards something, and most unhappily the one religious Communion among us which has of late years been practically in possession of this something is the Church of Rome. She alone, amid all the errors and evils of her practical system, has given free scope to the feelings of awe, mystery, tenderness, reverence, devotedness, and other feelings which may be especially called Catholic. The question, then, is, whether we shall give them up to the Roman Church, or claim them for ourselves, as we well may, by reverting to that older system, which has of late years indeed been superseded, but which has been, and is, quite congenial (to say the least), I should rather say proper and natural, or even necessary to the Church.' And here follow the significant words : ' But if we do give them up, then we must give up the men who cherish them. We must consent either to give up the men, or to admit their principles.'*

Before following the further course of the movement, it

---

* Letter addressed to the Rev. R. W. Jelf, D.D., Canon of Christ Church, in explanation of the 90th ' Tract for the Times,' by the author, 1841.

may be useful if I give a list of the Tracts and their authors, as compiled by Dean Burgon with the assistance of Archdeacon Harrison.

Of the *ninety* Tracts, *eighteen* are reprints from the writings of old English divines : viz., *twelve* (Nos. 37, 39, 42, 44, 46, 48, 50, 53, 55, 62, 65, 70) derived from the works of Bishop Wilson; *three* (Nos, 26, 27, 28) from Bishop Cosin; *one* (No. 25) from Bishop Beveridge ; *one* (No. 64) from Bishop Bull; *one* (No. 72) from Archbishop Ussher.

Four are Catenæ (Nos. 74, 76, 78, 81). The last was by Archdeacon Harrison, and had a Tract by Dr. Pusey prefixed.

Of the remaining *sixty-eight, twenty-seven* were by J. H. Newman (viz., Nos. 1, 2, 3, 6, 7, 8, 10, 11, 19, 20, 21, 31, 33, 34, 38, 41, 45, 47, 71, 73, 75, 79, 82, 83, 85, 88, 90). *Eight* by John Keble (Nos. 4, 13, 40, 52, 54, 57, 60, 89). *Six* by Dr. Pusey (Nos. 18, 66, 67, 68, 69, 77).

Four were by J. W. Bowden (Nos. 5, 29, 30, 56). *Four* by Thomas Keble (Nos. 12, 22, 43, 84). *Four* by Archdeacon Harrison (Nos. 16, 17, 24, 49).

Three were by the Hon. A. P. Perceval (Nos. 23, 35, 36). *Three* by R. H. Froude (Nos. 9, 59, 63). *Three* by Isaac Williams (Nos. 80, 86, 87).

One was by Alfred Menzies (No. 14); *one* by C. P. Eden (No. 32).

No. 15 was the joint production of W. Palmer and J. H. Newman. No. 51 is attributed to R. F. Wilson, but the authorship is uncertain. The authorship of Nos. 58 and 61 is unknown.

No. 8 is attributed above to Newman, but it is disputed whether he or Froude wrote it.

LECTURE IV.

THE OXFORD MOVEMENT (*continued*).

TRACT XC. fell upon Oxford and the religious world like a thunderbolt. It was published on February 27, 1841, and on the 8th of the following month four Senior Tutors addressed the editor, charging the Tract with suggesting a way to enable men to violate their engagements with the University.

On the 15th the Board of Heads of Houses met and published their judgment, without waiting for Mr. Newman's reply, which was known to be in the press, and which, when it eventually came out, was found to be dated March 13.

The judgment is as follows: 'At a meeting of the Vice-Chancellor, Heads of Houses, and Proctors in the Delegates' Room, March 15, 1841. Resolved—that the modes of interpretation, such as are suggested in the said Tract, evading rather than explaining the sense of the Thirty-nine Articles, and reconciling subscription to them with the adoption of errors, which they were designed to counteract, defeat the object, and are inconsistent with the due observance of the above-mentioned statutes.—P. WYNTER, Vice-Chancellor.'

At this crisis in the Church's history one feels quite sorry for the bishops of the time. On one hand we are told that, had their theology been more accurate and extensive, they would have seen that there was nothing in the Tractarian papers really inconsistent with the Prayer-Book and the authority of the best English divines, and had they extended their fatherly protection to the writers they might have steered the movement clear of its dangers, saved the seceders from leaving the Church, and shared in whatever credit may have been due to the revival. On the other hand they are severely blamed by their Protestant friends for not discerning the 'undoubted leanings' of the Tracts from the opening numbers, and for not nipping the incipient Popery in the bud. Thus the Rev. Daniel Wilson, in the 'Appeal' before quoted, says: 'Nor can the mournful fact be concealed that a want of due vigilance and faithfulness to the cause of Protestant truth was evinced at this period by many of those who might have exercised their authority in the Church for the suppression of these novel doctrines. The heresies which now threaten us might apparently have been nipped in the bud if our ecclesiastical rulers had united in a firm protest against them. It would be unbecoming in a mere presbyter to say more on this delicate subject. Difficulties of a peculiar nature doubtless presented themselves to any combined movement on the part of the Bench of Bishops. Still, the fact cannot be denied that the very step which some of the bishops were ready to adopt in protesting against the recent decision of the Privy Council was not taken to suppress the introduction of Romanizing principles into the Church. Many even of those bishops who in their public charges expressed their disapproval of these doctrines, mingled their admonitions with so many expressions of respect for the motives of the movement party, as greatly to weaken the effect of their reproof. Nor have the influential laity and leading parochial clergy been free from blame in this matter. With a few noble exceptions, there has been too much caution and reserve manifested by all parties.'

Whether the bishops were half persuaded by the cogent

reasoning of the Tracts, as it presented itself to their dormant theological sense, or whether, in the disturbed condition of the Church, they found it impossible to adopt any concerted action, they exhibited throughout the movement a good deal of that dignified apathy which was supposed to be the leading characteristic of their high station. But on this occasion, whatever they usually did, or abstained from doing, collectively, they agreed, almost to a man, with the decision of the Oxford Board, and the unfortunate Tract was pelted with anathemas from one Episcopal throne after another. Thus O'Brien, Bishop of Ossory:

'Throughout the whole Tract, the dishonest casuistry to which the Jesuits have given a name is employed upon a scale to which it would be hard to find a parallel, except in the more notorious of their own writings. I should despair of conveying anything like a full impression of the shifting, evasive, and disingenuous sophistry with which the purpose of the Tract is followed out.'

And: 'A mode of escape from the fair force of the most solemn and sacred obligations—by such sophistry and evasion, by such shifts and contrivances, as a man could not apply to the very lightest of the engagements of common life without forfeiting all reputation for integrity and good faith.'

Bagot, Bishop of Oxford:

'A system of interpretation which is so subtle that by it the Articles may be made to mean anything or nothing.'

Kaye, Bishop of Lincoln:

'It appears to me a proceeding inconsistent with religious sincerity, and calculated to deaden the perception of truth in the mind, both of him who puts forth such interpretations, and of them to whom they are addressed. What will be the ultimate result of the course pursued by the learned author of the Tract in question remains to be seen.'

Ponsonby, Bishop of Derry:

'It becomes your duty to guard the *inestimable treasure*,

which in her Articles our Church has handed down to us, from false interpolations.'

Mant, Bishop of Down and Connor and Dromore:

'A process for ascertaining the truth the very contrary to that which our Church has prescribed, the consequences of which must needs be the co-existence of subscription to the Articles with an inward belief of the very errors which the Articles themselves were framed to counteract.'*

Copleston, Bishop of Llandaff:

'Loose and dangerous doctrine; a dishonest course tending to corrupt the conscience and to destroy all confidence between man and man; a want of principle which ought to exclude the subscriber, not only from sacred functions, but from every office of important trust.'

Dr. Close, of Cheltenham (afterwards Dean of Carlisle):

'I should be sorry to trust the author of that Tract with my purse.'

Dr. Whately (then Archbishop of Dublin) seems to mingle his condemnation with a touch of irony at the Articles themselves:

'Neither the reformers of our Church nor any other human being could frame any expressions such as not to admit of being explained away, or the consequences of them somehow evaded, by an ingenious person, who should resolutely set himself to the task.'

In my last lecture I quoted from Newman himself as to the real object of the Tract, to which I may add the calm and unbiased opinion of Dean Church: 'It was anything but what it was taken to mean by the authorities—an intentional move in favour of Rome. It was intended to reconcile a large and growing class of minds, penetrated

* Though Bishop Jeremy Taylor, who occupied the same see some 200 years before, expresses himself thus: 'In such (*i.e.*, doubtful) cases let the Articles be made with as great latitude of sense as they can; and so that subscriptions be made to the form of words, let the subscribers understand them in what sense they please, which the truth of God will suffer, and the words can be capable of.'—'Ductor Dubitantium.'

and disgusted with the ignorance and injustice of much of the current controversial assumptions against Rome, to a larger and more defensible view of the position of the English Church. And this was done by calling attention to that which was not now for the first time observed—to the loose and unguarded mode of speaking visible in the later controversial Articles, and to the contrast between them and the technical and precise theology of the first five Articles. The Articles need not mean all which they were supposed popularly to mean against what was Catholic in Roman doctrine. This was urged in simple good faith; it was but the necessary assumption of all who held with the Catholic theology, which the Tractarians all along maintained that they had a right to teach; it left plenty of ground of difference with unreformed and usurping Rome.'*

Yet he admits that it was a mistake or miscalculation. Like all such bold declarations, while the Tract elicited plenty of venom from those who did not agree with it, it had the effect of drawing out many expressions of sympathy from those who were in advance of their time in their views about it. One notable instance was in the case of Dr. Walter Farquhar Hook, Vicar of Leeds, who writes as follows in a letter to his diocesan, the Bishop of Ripon: 'The moment I heard that Mr. Newman was to be silenced, not by argument, but by usurped authority, that moment I determined to renounce my intention of pointing out in Tract XC. what I considered to be its errors; that moment I determined to take my stand with Mr. Newman, because, though I did not approve of a particular Tract, yet in general principles—*in the very principle advocated in that Tract*—I did agree with him. In a word, I was compelled by circumstances to act as a party man. And in justice to one whom I am proud to call my friend, I am bound to say that Mr. Newman's explanatory letter to Dr. Jelf is, to my mind, perfectly satisfactory.'

* 'Oxford Movement,' ch. xv.

As this celebrated Tract brought the series to an end, and seems to mark a distinct epoch in the history of the Church of England, it may not be out of place here to take a brief survey of its influence on religious opinion :

In the first place, we notice that it draws a strong line of demarcation between the school which it represented and another school which had been rising at Oxford almost concurrently with it. Both schools were manifestations, in opposite directions, of that wholesome discontent with the state of things in general, and of religious things in particular, which could not but be felt by serious men of all shades of opinion. One school had supposed the remedies to lie in a recurrence to old principles which had been neglected, and as they considered those principles to have been damaged by the Reformation, they proposed a return to the authorities which had preceded that movement, or to those whose influence had been to moderate its extreme tendencies. The other school, speaking generally, were for commencing *de novo*, and reopening the question of the Divine idea about the Church, which they did not regard as satisfactorily realized either by Catholicism or Protestantism. On both sides, as must always be the case where men of strong personality are concerned, there was much difference of opinion in detail; but, on the whole, the Catholic school were more disposed to yield their personal views to a central authority, while their rivals were for the greater liberty of individualism.

Among the various theories of the Church put forth at the time there are three which require special notice. Mr. Ward's 'Ideal of a Christian Church,' which shall be considered later, illustrates the extreme view on one side; while two Oxford teachers—viz., Dr. Whately and Dr. Arnold—developed theories of their own, which, of course, differed immensely from Ward's 'Ideal,' but also differed very much from each other.

The 'Letters of an Episcopalian,' published in 1826,

exhibit Dr. Whately's conception of the Church as an organized society introduced into the world by Christ Himself, endued with definite spiritual powers, and, whether connected with the State or not, having an independent existence and inalienable claims with its own moral standard, and spirit, and character. Dr. Arnold's idea was far simpler. He divided the world into Christians and non-Christians, the former believing in, and worshipping, Christ, the mere fact of their doing so constituting them into a church (or society) in what he understood to be the sense of the word in the New Testament.

To put it briefly, the former of these Churches was a visible and tangible, the latter an invisible and purely spiritual, body. They differed obviously from each other, but both were alike, and both differed from the Tractarian view in these points: First, in neither scheme did it matter much about individual beliefs; secondly, in neither of them were the sacraments a necessity; thirdly, although both recognised the need of a clergy, it was rather as *teachers* than *priests* that they were regarded. In other words, they excluded, or reduced the importance of, what the Tractarians considered essential—viz., religious dogma, sacraments, and a sacerdotal system. Those who held the views of Dr. Whately and Dr. Arnold eventually merged into what is known as the Broad Church school, with which we associate such names as Stanley, Maurice, and Kingsley.

It will be obvious to the impartial student that both this and the school against which it was a reaction hold the truth between them. Either view of the Church, if held exclusively, is capable of being pushed to a pernicious extreme. Each is a wholesome correction of the other. And now that we have passed beyond the circumstances which brought these different opinions into violent contrast, many good Churchmen can see their way to hold them conjointly in such combination and proportion as to preserve at once the integrity of the Catholic faith and the liberty and independence of the individual. In its ordinary state, the co-existence of opposite schools of thought, within certain limits, is a condition of the Church's healthy life and activity. But at great crises of its history one will naturally become more important than the other, according to the peculiar evils of the time which it, and not its rival, will be the more likely to counteract.

Among the religious phenomena of the present day we have to count the reconciliation of opinions which were thought irreconcilable in 1841. At that date one of the most obvious results of Tract XC. was to draw out clearly the distinction between opposite schools of thought, each of which regarded its rival as hostile to the interests of the Church to which both belonged.

The Broad Church school, like the Tractarian, was a result of that 'Spirit in the air' to which reference has already been made. Each gained a certain intensity or suffered certain modifications from the proximity of the other. The tendencies of each were, in fact, driven further by the antagonism of its rival than would have been the case had both been very weak, or had either been sufficiently strong to exclude the other from the field. It would lead us too far from our immediate subject to follow the course of such individuals on either side as realized the extreme tendencies of their party. But this much may be said: On one hand, the celebrated papers called 'Essays and Reviews' show us the direction in which one set of opinions was going; on the other hand, we see the conservative and mediæval tendencies leading others beyond the lines originally contemplated in the revival, leading them, in fact, to leave the Church of their baptism for the Roman Communion.

If we had asked, Why? we should have received one answer, and one only, at the time: 'The Tractarian Movement could logically lead them nowhere else. This had been foreseen from the first.' But at this distance we can afford to look at the matter fairly, and shall be disposed to give weight to the following considerations:

In the first place, as has been already observed, the tendency of every movement is to drive men strongly in one direction, with the result that some are naturally carried further than others. We have an illustration in point, in the case of that very clever, though very eccentric, man, Mr. W. G. Ward, whose nature was of that ardent, impetuous sort, which may lead a man to do great things, but which prevents him from being a philosopher. This led him, while yet in the English Church, to break out into a criticism of her system and an exposure of her weak points, which we could better have understood from an enemy. It was an instance probably of a man of keen susceptibilities smarting under certain grievances, and, as usual in such cases, speaking out freely everything that was in his mind, without weighing his words, without considering their effect on others. The work in which this undutiful spirit is exhibited is his 'Ideal of a Christian Church,' published in 1844, of which a writer in the *Tablet* (a Romish paper) observes:

'It is a volume distinguished for its abhorrence of every shred of Protestantism, for deep sympathy with the Roman Church, for disgust and loathing at the present condition, theoretical and practical, of the Establishment. But of all its distinguishing features, we confess that we can find none more eminent than this—the extraordinary capacity of the author for standing upright and balancing himself on an invisible point, for walking in perfect sincerity upon a line, compared with which the edge of the keenest razor is breadth unlimited.'

Readers of Mr. Ward's interesting biography, lately published, will have no difficulty in finding parallels for his eccentric Churchmanship in other parts of his attractive but erratic disposition. In judging Mr. Ward, or anyone else who deviated from the 'sober standard of feeling,' which

Keble tells us is the ordinary result of the teaching of the Church of England, we must remember that the circumstances of the time were provocative of anything but sober feelings in sensitive people. Men are apt to say unpleasant things when they are angry. Still, one cannot help regarding Mr. Ward as an illustration of that wayward and capricious following which Newman himself regrets as always attached to a movement party : 'persons who talk loudly and strangely, do odd or fierce things, display themselves unnecessarily, and disgust other people.'

The great Cardinal himself illustrates another class of mind, influenced by the same circumstances, probably feeling them as keenly, but behaving very differently. Nothing is more striking in the history of the movement than his self-suppression under every form of provocation, and the uniform calmness of his language. It is a remarkable case of obedience under difficulties. His example in the matter of yielding to authority, and in respectful and temperate language when speaking of or to his ecclesiastical superiors (men vastly inferior to himself) is very touching, and might well have been followed by some of his successors. He resembled Mr. Ward, however, in taking that irrevocable step which has been a permanent loss to the Church of England.

The story of his conversion has been told by himself in the fascinating pages of his 'Apologia.' The growth and development of his religious opinions as there narrated is one of the most absorbing psychological studies in the English language. The turning-point in his career was briefly this : In the year 1831 he was invited to contribute a volume to the Theological Library about to be published by Mr. Rivington. His contribution was to be called 'The History of the Principal Councils.' The series was to consist of handy little volumes, uniform, aud with suitable embellishments. Newman, who had not yet won any considerable literary reputation, willingly undertook the task, which was never fulfilled in the form intended. But in 1833 Newman's labours revealed themselves in 'The History of the Arians,' containing the account of a *single council*, which, however, was more than enough for the limits prescribed. It was while pursuing his investigations on this subject, which naturally took him into the study of the early heresies, that he saw what he describes as *the ghost* which alarmed him about the English Church, and eventually took him to Rome. It was nothing more nor less than the identification of the Anglican Church, as dating from the Reformation, with certain early heretical sects, who, as he thought, had similarly cut themselves off from the Catholic body. However excellent the Church of England might be, the mere fact of her separation from the central authority was enough, in his view, to make her a mere sect. On the other hand, he had all along been impressed with the greatness of the Roman Church; formerly it had impressed him with the greatness of Antichrist; now it was impressive with the greatness of a wonderful system, commanding from the extent and imperial authority of its dominion, mysterious in its organization, influence, devotion, and claims to infallibility. As a member of the Church of England, he was of course alive to its defects, and he probably thought he had discovered in the Roman system, of whose interior working and evils he was necessarily ignorant, a *certainty*, whereas the Anglican was at best a doubtful expedient. The fact is, his mind was *too logical* to be satisfied with the anomalous compromise which the Church of this country, and at that time, appeared to present. He was struck with the spectacle of external completeness, with the logical and consistent position which the Church of Rome appeared to hold. He had taken in a part, an important part, but not the *whole*, of a great subject. He failed to take account of the whole range of Church and secular history, and to make allowances for the imperfections and inconsistencies which must be found in *any* church, and for the diversities of mind and character which lead men to take different views and different courses, which must be provided for in comparing one branch of the Church with another, and which, in an important sense, are as Divine as the Church itself. In other words, the actual working Church must always fall short here and there, if we look at it over an extended period, of the Divine ideal, or the theoretical Church ; and in this respect the Church of Rome, to those who know her intimately, appears as likely to have forfeited her privileges as our own.

These are suggested as typical of the motives which led two classes of people to Rome. Between them there would of course be any number of others, too numerous to classify, as varying with the circumstances and state of mind of individuals. There were intellectual and devotional wants of various kinds operating separately or together to lead people where they thought they should be satisfied. But as far as I have been able to discover, there were no secessions worth mentioning on those childish inducements which occur at once to the vulgar mind—*e.g.*, the love of theatrical effect in the act of secession, the morbid excitement of disturbing friendships, or the attractions of music, relics, flowers, candles, rosaries, and other accessories of worship which make up the popular idea of Romanism. In the case of Mr. Newman the step was carefully weighed, long deferred, and only taken at the expense of such self-abnegation and mental suffering as are a complete guarantee of its sincerity. The secessions, which were the result of his example, would appear to have been equally deliberate, that is, in the mental process which preceded the final act. Such an act would always appear sudden and unaccountable to those who had not been taken into the confidence of the seceders during their uncertainties and anxieties. But even in the more impulsive cases there is no reason to suspect people of insincerity. As a matter of fact, in every case worth mentioning there was everything to lose in a worldly sense—social advantages, chances of promotion, and so forth—the gain being entirely of a spiritual and personal nature. It was a 'venture of faith' from the point of view of the person concerned. On the whole, it is impossible to avoid the conclusion that, had the authorities in Oxford and the Church shown a more conciliatory and intelligent spirit, the wave of secession might have been arrested.

'Was it wonderful,' Dean Church observes, 'when men were told that the Church of England was no place for them, that they were breaking their vows and violating solemn engagements by acting as its ministers, and that in order to preserve the respect of honest men they should leave it, that the question of change, far off as it had once seemed, came within "measurable distance"? The generation to which they belonged had been brought up with strong exhortations to be real and to hate shams; and now the question was forced on them whether it was not a sham for the English Church to call itself Catholic; whether a body of teaching which was denounced by its authorities, however it might look on paper and be defended by learning, could be more than a plausible literary hypothesis in contrast to the great working system of which the head was Rome. When we consider the singular and anomalous position on any theory, including the Roman, of the English Church, with what great differences its various features and elements have been prominent at different times, how largely its history has been marked by contradictory facts and appearances, and how hard it is for anyone to keep all, according to their real importance, simultaneously in view; when we remember, also, what are the temptations of human nature in great collisions of religious belief, the excitement and passion of the time, the mixed character of all religious zeal, the natural inevitable anger which accompanies it when resisted, the fervour which welcomes self-sacrifice for the truth ; and when we think of all this kept aglow by the continuous provocation of unfair and harsh dealing from persons who were scarcely entitled to be severe judges, the wonder is, human nature being what it is, not that so many went, but that so many stayed.'*

Whatever we may think now of Tract XC. and the 'Ideal of a Church,' there can be no doubt that their publication was prejudicial to the movement by raising suspicions which might have been set at rest by works of a more guarded and conciliatory nature. Whether the same amount of permanent good would have resulted is open to question. But these works certainly postponed the work of the movement, and alienated certain moderate men who had hitherto been friendly, but who were unable to follow the writers in their rapid advance. They were an injury to the movement inflicted on itself, though, of course, intensified by the public condemnation which followed on their publication.

In addition to the mischief wrought from within, the Tractarians were to suffer two blows from without, which form part of the history of the movement, and must be briefly noticed. In 1841 Keble vacated the Poetry Professorship, and in a competition for the vacancy between Isaac Williams and Mr. Garbett the latter was elected by a majority of three votes to two. Mr. Garbett is spoken of as a gentleman of high culture, and with some acquaintance with foreign literature, then a rare accomplishment in the University, but he had given no evidence whatever of his poetical qualifications. Mr. Williams had shown in his 'Baptistery' that he *was* a poet, and was capable of using his gifts for the same high ends as those which Keble and Wordsworth had always kept in view, namely, the elevation of character and the inculcation of religious and moral teaching. The contest, however, did not turn on the literary knowledge or poetical gifts of the competitors, but on the question of Church principles, and Mr. Williams had

* 'Oxford Movement,' ch. xv.

been identified with the advanced guard of the unpopular party since the publication of his Tracts on Reserve. I have already said something about those papers. As regards the man himself, he is described as retiring and modest to a fault, who could scarcely see a dozen people together without wishing to hide himself. But it was his misfortune to expose himself to popular indignation as the author of the first really objectionable paper in the series, unfortunate in its title, and supposed to embody all the secret aims of the party. It was owing to the well-meant but injudicious intervention of Dr. Pusey that the contest was carried on and decided on religious grounds, and the consequence was that Isaac Williams was defeated by a man who could not write a line of poetry. Under the circumstances the defeat extended to the party who had supported the unsuccessful candidate. It was looked upon by them and their opponents as a public condemnation of principles which both sides felt to be at stake.

The second external blow to the movement was the suspension of Dr. Pusey for a period of two years on the ground of the doctrine said to be contained in his sermon on 'The Holy Eucharist a Comfort to the Penitent,' preached at Christ Church on the 4th Sunday after Easter (May 24), 1843. The story has been told at some length, and, I believe, for the first time, in Dean Church's admirable work on the movement. It will be sufficient to say here that the whole proceeding savours of unfairness and irregularity, and most people would now regard the grounds of the suspension as insufficient. His judges carefully abstained from pointing out the particular passage or passages in which the objectionable doctrine was conveyed, but based their censure on the general tone of the sermon, which they seem to have regarded as approaching dangerously near to the scholastic theory. As Dr. Pusey states in his preface, he was conscious of his own entire adherence to the formularies of the English Church, and having guarded against misconception at the outset by expressing his belief that the elements 'remained in their natural substances,' and avoiding any definition of the mode in which the mystery was brought about, he had no fear of being misunderstood. The sermon was devotional rather than controversial, and was fully in accord with the sentiment of the judicious Hooker, 'that men should more give themselves to meditate with silence what we have by the Sacrament, and less to dispute of the manner how.' But Dr. Pusey could not honestly have expressed anything short of that doctrine of the Real Presence which he held in common with the most authoritative Anglican divines.

The sacred nature of the subject precluded an argumentative treatment in the sermon itself, but the question having been raised, it was published with an appendix, which abundantly supported the author's position by quotations from the 'Homily on the Sacrament,' Bishop Ridley, Hooker, Overall, Andrewes, Dr. Donne, Sutton, Laud, Bishop Forbes, Archbishop Bramhall, Cosin, Sparrow, Hammond, Thorndike, Jeremy Taylor, Bishop Ken, Beveridge, Bull, Hickes, Comber, Wilson, and others.

Perhaps the best comment on the transaction is the fact that Dr. Pusey was in due time restored, without having uttered or written a word which could be considered as a retractation. On the 4th Sunday after Epiphany, 1846, he again preached before the University. The sermon on the 'Entire Absolution of the Penitent' has now become historical. I should have said that in the former sermon the Holy Eucharist was specially considered as a means of conveying pardon. And now, on his restoration to the pulpit, Dr. Pusey takes up the thread of his subject precisely at the point where he left it about three years before in words which, in spite of their solemnity, are apt to provoke a smile at the irony they contain. 'It will be in the memory of some,' he says, 'that when, nearly three years past, Almighty God (for "secret faults" which He knoweth, and from which, I trust, He willed thereby the rather to "cleanse" me) allowed me to be deprived for a time of this my office among you, I was endeavouring to mitigate the stern doctrine of the heavy character of a Christian's sins by pointing out the mercies of God,' etc. 'And now, brethren, I would proceed to speak of that great authoritative act whereby God in the Church still forgives the sins of the penitent.'

In the second sermon no attempt was made to explain any misconceptions which might have been raised by the first; much less was there any withdrawal of the doctrine therein set forth. One sermon is merely the continuation and complement of the other. If the comparison be not irreverent, these sermons may be regarded as the Alpha and Omega of the movement, for they contain the two fundamental doctrines to whose neglect the Church of England owed its debasement, and to whose restoration the Tractarians naturally looked for a recovery of its life and vigour, namely, a higher view of the Sacraments (especially that of the Lord's Supper), and a higher view of the position and responsibilities of the clergy to whose ministration the Sacraments had been entrusted. The suspension of Dr. Pusey was a temporary blow to the movement, and showed that at the particular time the doctrines at stake were not those of the official representatives of the Church; but it is not too much to say that he who stated them so courageously has so far gained his point that, even if his teaching is not generally held, it stands on too secure a basis of authority and practice to be ever again ignored.

That the Tractarians were right in their view of the root of evil in the Church is evident from the revival of religion which has followed on their teaching. That their anticipations have been more than realized I hope to show in my last lecture. The Oxford Movement has been, in a very real sense, the salvation of the Church of England. Though retarded by the events I have just tried to relate, the revival was not frustrated ; its enemies thought it was not seriously interrupted.*

* 'The clear and logical style (of the Tracts) attracted the reader. The earnestness and devotion of the writers gave confidence . . . . the influence of Mr. Newman and Dr. Pusey rapidly increased. The sermons of the former at St. Mary's, Oxford, on the Sunday afternoons, were precisely calculated to awaken doubts in the minds of his auditors in reference to the distinctive doctrines of the Reformation. . . . The series of Oxford Tracts came to a sudden close at the suggestion of the diocesan. But this was merely a change in the mode of assault ; the efforts against Protestant truth were redoubled. The silencing of Dr. Pusey in the University pulpit, and the condemnation of Mr. Ward's book, hardly served to check for a moment the rising tide. The *British Critic*, and other similar publications, became the recognised organs of the party, and enabled them in a still more unblushing manner, under the cover of anonymous authorship, to insult the Reformation.'—' Our Protestant Faith in Danger ' : Rev. Daniel Wilson.

LECTURE V.

THE LITERATURE OF THE CATHOLIC REVIVAL.

EVERY great movement naturally has its own peculiar features. If the movement we are now considering is distinguished in any way from others, it is in its intellectual and literary character. There was nothing popular about it; it made no appeal to the senses, nor availed itself of any of those oratorical, emotional, or exciting means by which the masses are most directly, if not most effectually, reached. To use Lord Macaulay's words (applied to a different subject), it 'moved the intellects which have moved the world,' and it moved them by the persuasive force and logic of its writings. In saying this I hope I shall not be supposed to ignore the religious impulse which lay at the root of the movement, and was, of course, the ultimate cause of its success. If, however, the Tractarians had been mere religious enthusiasts they might have done a great work in the Church and have left an impression on their age, but the results would have been different. They would not have affected the same class of people; their work might have permeated society from below upwards, but I question whether it would ultimately have been so extensive or so permanent. There are obviously two ways of affecting society. It may be done (*has* been done) by bringing together large masses of people, and by powerful addresses or other external excitements stirring them up to act as one man. Popular movements of this kind are always attended with considerable danger, and are very apt to defeat their own object. But this mode of reviving public interest was precluded by the very nature of the subject. The alternative was to work, as it were, from the centre towards the circumference. The very nature of the great actors in the revival made this the only possible method, and in pursuing it they had before them the example of the Founder of Christianity, Who, beginning with a few chosen disciples, gradually enlarged the circle of His influence till His teaching was extended over the earth as the 'waters cover the sea.' The real work of the movement was not done at large public meetings, unless a devout congregation here and there in church can be so called, but in the hearts and brains of thoughtful people, in the quiet and solitude of studies and libraries. In its later stages, as the circle of its influence extended, the revival naturally altered its character, and became more exoteric in its teaching and its methods. But its original force lay in its religious literature; and all through the Oxford Movement, properly so called, *i.e.*, from 1833 to 1845, its work was chiefly done by the pens of the writers associated with it, and by the quiet work in their parishes of those who championed its opinions. If this movement had done nothing else, it would still have rendered the Church an invaluable service in the writings of its leaders and supporters—nay, in much of the writings of its opponents, whether for a controversial or independent character—for it is pretty certain that the pens of opposite or divergent schools were set in motion by the questions raised in the 'Tracts for the Times.'

I have already said all that was necessary about these celebrated papers in tracing the course of the movement. In point of importance one is naturally obliged to give them the first place. *Next* to them in importance, but *before* them in a literary sense, the place of honour must be given to those wonderful sermons preached by Mr. Newman at the four o'clock services on Sunday afternoons at St. Mary's,

Oxford. In some respects these sermons were even more important than the Tracts, for it is doubtful whether the movement would have gone on without them; it is quite certain that without them it would not have been what it was. 'Even people who heard them continually,' Dean Church observes, 'and felt them to be different from any other sermons, hardly estimated their real power, or knew at the time the influence which the sermons were having upon them. Plain, direct, unornamented, clothed in English that was only pure and lucid, free from any faults of taste, strong in their flexibility and perfect command both of language and thought, they were the expression of a piercing and large insight into character and conscience and motives, of a sympathy at once most tender and most stern with the tempted and the wavering, of an absolute and burning faith in God and His counsels, in His love, in His judgments, in the awful glory of His generosity and His magnificence. They made men think of the things which the preacher spoke of, and not of the sermon or the preacher. Since 1828 this preaching had been going on at St. Mary's, growing in purpose and directness as the years went on, though it could hardly be more intense than in some of its earliest examples. While men were reading and talking about the Tracts, they were hearing the sermons; and in the sermons they heard the living meaning, and reason, and bearing of the Tracts, their ethical affinities, their moral standard. The sermons created a moral atmosphere, in which men judged the questions in debate.'*

* Oxford Movement.—The late Principal J. C. Shairp, Professor of Humanity, St. Andrew's, a Presbyterian, describes Newman's preaching thus:

'The centre from which his power went forth was the pulpit of St. Mary's, with those wonderful afternoon sermons. Sunday after Sunday, year by year, they went on, each continuing and deepening the impression produced by the last. As the hour interfered with the dinner-hour of the colleges, most men preferred a warm dinner without Newman's sermon to a cold one with it; so the audience was not crowded—the

I strongly recommend everyone who has not read these sermons to set to work and read them forthwith. 'The

large church little more than half filled. The service was very simple—no pomp, no ritualism ; for it was characteristic of the leading men of the movement that they left these things to the weaker brethren. Their thoughts, at all events, were set on great questions which touched the heart of unseen things. About the service the most remarkable thing was the beauty, the silver intonation of Mr. Newman's voice as he read the lessons. When he began to preach a stranger was not likely to be much struck. Here was no vehemence, no declamation, no show of elaborate argument, so that one who came prepared to hear "a great intellectual effort" was almost sure to go away disappointed. . . . Those who never heard him might fancy that his sermons would generally be about Apostolical succession, or rights of the Church, or against Dissenters. Nothing of the kind. You might hear him preach for weeks without an allusion to these things. What there was of High Church teaching was implied rather than enforced. The local, the temporary and the modern were ennobled by the presence of the Catholic truth belonging to all ages that pervaded the whole. His power showed itself chiefly in the new and unlooked-for way in which he touched into life old truths, moral or spiritual, which all Christians acknowledge, but most have ceased to feel ; when he spoke of "unreal words," of the "individuality of the soul," of the "invisible world," of a "particular Providence"; or, again, of the "ventures of faith," "warfare the condition of victory," "the Cross of Christ the measure of the world," "the Church a home for the lonely." As he spoke, how the old truth became new ! how it came home with a meaning never felt before ! He laid his finger, how gently, yet how powerfully, on some inner place in the hearer's heart, and told him things about himself he had never known till then. Subtlest truths, which it would have taken philosophers pages of circumlocution and big words to state, were dropped out by the way in a sentence or two of the most transparent Saxon. What delicacy of style, yet what strength ! how simple, yet how suggestive ! how homely, yet how refined ! how penetrating, yet how tender-hearted ! If now and then there was a forlorn undertone which at the time seemed inexplicable, you might be perplexed at the drift of what he said, but you felt all the more drawn to the speaker. . . . After hearing these sermons, you might come away still not believing the tenets peculiar to the High Church system ; but you would be harder than most men if you did not feel more than ever ashamed of coarseness, selfishness, worldliness ; if you did not feel the things of faith brought closer to the soul.'

Parochial and Plain Sermons,' as they are called, are published in eight volumes, the first six containing the author's Parochial Sermons, the seventh and eighth his contribution to the series of Plain Sermons by certain contributors to the 'Tracts for the Times.'*

I recommend people to read them wherever I have a chance, not only in connection with the study of the religious movement which they so distinctly furthered, but for these reasons: first, as models of English composition; secondly, for their philosophical and moral value—they are far from being dry dogmatic discourses; thirdly, because if a person had read nothing else in theology he would find in them a very good Churchman's education; and, lastly, because I have personally felt the weight of their influence in the formation of character and opinion. Most people who have been influenced by books at all can point to certain favourite works which have left a deeper impression than others. If I thought that my own experience was at all peculiar, I should not mention it in public; but most people will probably agree with me in the ethical value of Bacon's 'Essays,' Jeremy Taylor's 'Holy Living and Dying,' Milton's 'Paradise Lost,' Dante's 'Divine Comedy.' To these many will be disposed to add Newman's 'Sermons.' Perhaps a few 'opinions of the press,' from papers of very different opinions in other matters, will be interesting from their agreement on this subject.

The *Nonconformist* says: 'In reading these sermons, it is impossible to withhold one's high admiration for the many fine qualities which they display: plain, unambiguous statement of Christian doctrine according to the preacher's view of it; practical application of Church dogmas to individual life, character and conduct; instructive exposition

---

* They are now to be had at the low price of 3s. 6d. a volume in Messrs. Longman's Silver Library, the only objection to which is the binding, which seems unsuitable for theological books.

of Scripture—all conveyed in a faultless style and with well-sustained eloquence.'

The *Pall Mall Gazette*: 'They are undeniably models of style in writing of the most faultless kind. As addresses to a miscellaneous multitude, they would have been failures; but as addresses to a cultivated audience of University students and tutors, they are without a rival.'

The *Saturday Review*: 'Dr. Newman's sermons stand by themselves in modern English literature; it might be said in English literature generally. There have been equally great masterpieces of English writing in this form of composition, and there have been preachers whose theological depth, acquaintance with the heart, earnestness, tenderness and power have not been inferior to his. But the great writers do not touch, pierce, and get hold of minds as he does, and those who are famous for the power and results of their preaching do not write as he does. His sermons have done more, perhaps, than any one thing to mould and quicken and brace the religious temper of our time; they have acted with equal force on those who were nearest and those who were furthest from him in theological opinion.'

These and many other notices to the same effect might be illustrated by any number of quotations from the sermons. The matchless clearness and vigour of the style would naturally make them admired by literary men, and will secure them a permanent place among the great masters of our language. It is probable that they have done more for the Catholic Revival than any other writings of the same school, and they have probably had a wider influence among people more or less opposed to it. The reason, I think, is that the doctrines which run through them are seldom brought into painful prominence as dogmatic certainties, but are stated with a sort of polite hesitation, as an educated gentleman might be expected to state them in conversation with an opponent, though, at the same time, they are supported by an elaborateness of argument which makes them almost irresistible. And they exhibit a profound and extensive knowledge of character such as one might rather expect from a man of the world than from a student and recluse, who must necessarily have spent more time among books and in the offices of religion than in general society.

There are passages in them which for practical wisdom and insight into motive might well make up a text-book for the guidance of a man of business. The fact is that, like most other great writings, they are to a great extent autobiographical. The discussions and arguments are not merely the *imaginationes ad libitum* of one who was beating the air, but are those which the author himself passed through in arriving at a solution of the difficulties under review. This makes them particularly valuable to intellectual people, who are more disposed to accept a probable suggestion than a definite dogmatic statement on any question incapable of mathematical demonstration. Where, however, the subject is settled for the author by the authority of the Bible or the Church, the truth, as he conceived it, is fearlessly stated.

The strength of Dr. Newman's sermons and of his other writings lies in the fact that he was no mere theologian, but had had a very wide reading in secular literature. His knowledge of Gibbon, for instance, is proverbial; and it is said that he had made an immense number of extracts from that historian, whole passages from whom he could recite word for word. It should be said that he very seldom introduces a quotation into his sermons, and they are quite remarkable for the absence of illustrations or images, as I believe they are technically called. In this respect these sermons are the very antipodes of those of Jeremy Taylor, every other line of which is a quotation or poetical image. You will notice that every sermon in the collection has a title giving the key to its contents, though most of them contain much collateral matter which could not be inferred from the titles. Bishop Wilberforce attributed the popularity of the sermons to this practice of the author's, and I think he goes on to say that he was the first preacher who adopted the practice. He must mean among modern preachers, for it is not unknown in old sermons. Those of Bishop Taylor, for instance, are a case in point.

Those who have read Newman's sermons will want to read more; and, as is not always the case, even with the most celebrated writers, almost everything that he wrote is worth reading, whether one is entirely persuaded by his teaching or not. His 'Essays on Miracles,' 'Historical Sketches,' 'Apologia,' and 'Grammar of Assent' are all worth careful study, besides his pretty little historical story of 'Callista'—a picture of the Church in North Africa in the third century. With one exception,* I have not yet read any of the Cardinal's sermons in the Church of Rome, but I am told that they exhibit a greater freedom of style than those he preached in the Anglican Communion; they are quoted as less classically severe, but not so destitute of illustrations.

But I must not forget his poems, especially the 'Dream of Gerontius,' which, according to Edmund Yates, unfolds a more vivid picture of the invisible world than anything in literature since the time of Dante. Some years ago Mr. Yates wrote a series of sketches in the *World* on 'Celebrities at Home,' in which such different personalities as Mr. Spurgeon, Ouida the novelist, and Cardinal Newman are exhibited in private life. The writer's visit to the oratory at Edgbaston is very interesting, and sets the Cardinal before us, as it were, in the flesh, and tells us of his relaxations, such as playing on the violin, and his love of a good novel. His favourite novelists are said to have been Sir

* The funeral sermon preached at the Requiem Mass for Mr. Hope-Scott, at the Church of the Immaculate Conception, Farm Street, on May 5, 1873.

Walter Scott, Thackeray, and Mrs. Gaskell. There is one anecdote which shows his humility: After he had written the 'Dream of Gerontius,' he thought so little of it that he pitched it into a waste-paper basket, from which it was rescued by one of the brethren, who thought it deserved a better fate. You will remember that the beautiful hymn, 'Praise to the Holiest in the height,' is taken from this poem. It is touching to recollect that the 'Dream' was an inseparable pocket-companion with General Gordon; and after his death it was sent by a relative to the Cardinal, who was deeply moved by the General's notes in the margin, showing the value he set upon the little book.

You will remember a few years ago there was a discussion about the 'best hundred books.' In giving his opinion on the subject, Professor Ruskin had marked Scott, '*Read every word.*' Whatever people may profess to think about the great novelist, I am afraid there are very few who carry out Ruskin's advice literally. Life is probably too short to read 'every word' of any author; but if there is one more than another who might be so read without waste of time, I should be disposed to say his name was Newman.*

I fear that I must dismiss Keble's and Pusey's sermons, which also belong to the literature of the movement, more briefly. Keble's are interesting, and, as we should expect from a writer of his poetical mind, they contain many beautiful illustrations. But if there is one thing that strikes us more than another in reading them, it is the self-suppression under which the author apparently labours, probably from a conscientious obligation to simplify his thoughts and language so as to keep well within the comprehension of his hearers. The English is, of course,

---

* As illustrating the decline in Scott, there is a little anecdote in Professor Ornsby's 'Memoirs of Mr. J. R. Hope-Scott,' to the effect that one of the Fathers at the Birmingham Oratory had actually found it necessary to offer a prize for the getting up of 'Kenilworth,' to induce the youths under education there to read it, so tedious has Scott become to the present generation.

classically pure, but one misses that piercing insight into life and character, as well as those fascinating philosophical passages which rivet the mind in Newman. It seems that Newman was incapable of suppressing himself entirely. The opening of his sermons is often extremely simple, but as the subject develops the author seems unconsciously led away by his thoughts into deeper profundities than he at first had in view; consequently the sermons, with the plainest possible beginning, become the most elaborate as the leading thought is pursued through all its ramifications in the writer's mind. Keble, on the other hand, seems always under the dominion of some restraining influence, as if his congregation and their practical benefit were before him throughout. It must be admitted, of course, that Keble's intellect was less piercing and comprehensive than that of his great compeer; and it is also necessary to remember that the two preachers as a rule were addressing entirely different congregations. Had they changed places, it is probable that neither would have been so successful. As far as Keble's prose writings are concerned, he is probably at his best in those miscellaneous essays which involve a combination of secular with religious considerations, and where the author felt himself free to give play to his thoughts and language. The review of Lockhart's 'Life of Scott,' written for the *British Critic* in 1838, is an excellent specimen of his style in this direction.

His essays have been reprinted as a collection, and for the reason I have suggested they are much more interesting reading than his sermons. Of course, a preacher's first duty is to his parishioners, and a sermon otherwise highly entertaining and instructive as an intellectual feat might be utterly useless as regards those who heard it. Keble's main object was the religious education of a village congregation.

His 'Letters of Spiritual Counsel' are very instructive, containing as they do the results of his wide experience as a spiritual guide. It is hardly necessary to say that a revival of the Catholic idea of the priestly office would be followed as a necessary consequence by a revival of the practice of auricular confession; but even before this had become at all general those who were in any way known to favour it were consulted very largely in cases of conscience, even by those who fell short of the complete Sacramental idea. I suppose there is in every mind a desire for some *particeps curarum*, either of a parental or sacerdotal character; and the enunciation of the doctrine of penance and absolution met with a response in many quarters where grief had been silently endured simply because no suitable outlet had been revealed for it. The leaders of the movement had their full share of sacred confidences; and after the secession of Newman the full weight of this kind of consultation naturally fell on Mr. Keble and Dr. Pusey.

The correspondence of both men in this way alone was simply enormous. The experience derived from it is exhibited in a general way in their writings, but Keble embodied the results of his experience in the letters referred to, or rather selected such cases as he judged to be of general interest, for I believe none of the letters are purely imaginary. They were all on questions actually raised by living correspondents, to whom the originals had been addressed.

To turn to Dr. Pusey: the feature about his sermons which perhaps first strikes the ordinary reader is their great length, which is very remarkable in these days of short sermons. It is worth noticing, in passing, that we are indebted to certain followers of the revival for an abbreviation of the average length of the sermon—possibly on the example of Dr. Newman, whose discourses seldom exceed ten or twelve pages. Pusey's were considerably longer, and if it had not been for the preacher's impressive voice and manner they would not have been endured. Sir F. Doyle tells us in a humorous way that he had a grudge against the doctor in this matter, as he generally made him late for dinner. 'Pusey's voice,' says Mozley, 'might want music and flexibility, but whatever the cause, it was a powerful engine. A man with a harsh, or rumbling, or husky, or squeaky voice, preaching those sermons, would never have been listened to.'*

The reason why these sermons are so long I believe to be—not that Dr. Pusey had no time to make them shorter, but simply that, whatever subject he dealt with, he was obliged, from the nature of his mind, to develop it to its fullest extent, to look at it from every point, to justify completely 'the ways of God to man.' It seems as if Dr. Pusey could not write a short paper. It has been already mentioned that from the time of his active connection with the 'Tracts for the Times' there was a manifest difference in their size. From short, pithy papers, such as tracts are usually supposed to be, they became elaborate treatises, Pusey's contributions taking the lead in this respect. His Tract on baptism covers several hundred pages, and, as Dean Church remarks, is by far the most complete exposition of the subject which has yet appeared in the English language. Still, if one has the patience to read them, Pusey's sermons will be found very rewarding. They contain a valuable body of theology, in whose composition the author's rich stores of knowledge, from the Fathers to modern German writers, are displayed. But the enormous range of his studies formed the same sort of impediment in his case as in that of many distinguished German theologians; his movements were hampered thereby, and his sermons lack that easy arrangement often exhibited by men of far less information.

There is a linguistic defect, too, that one notices, which also seems due to the writer's extensive acquisitions. I think it was at the early age of twenty-eight that he became Regius Professor of Hebrew. To this he added other

* 'Reminiscences of Oriel.'

Oriental as well as the European languages. I cannot help thinking that his English suffers from this embarrassment of riches. The complexities of foreign grammars and foreign modes of expression obtruded themselves on his English composition, making it somewhat heavy, so that one feels again and again as if it is a translation rather than a piece of original writing that one is reading. In other words, had he been less learned, his English would probably have been more readable.

But the charm, the power of Dr. Pusey's discourses depends on other, and far higher, qualities than those of mere words and arrangement. There is his fatherly manner —'My sons' is his favourite way of addressing the Oxford men—a manner springing out of his sympathy and love of others. There is his deep spiritual insight into their minds and souls. He had the virtues of a confessor—viz., that sweet disposition which attracts people to unbosom their secrets, the grace to console, and the knowledge to guide them in difficulties. His sermons are the result of a profound and extensive acquaintance with human weakness and human capabilities, combined with a lively sense of the Divine presence and co-operation in human affairs. God and the soul is their keynote. If it be not irreverent to allocate the three Oxford leaders to the Trinity of man's being, I should say that Pusey answered to the *soul*, Newman to the *mind*, and Keble to the *body*—that is, as the poet of nature, by recognising and elevating the physical. By a little stretch of allegory it could be shown that this division corresponds with their respective parts in the revival.

This leads me to say something about the poetry of the movement. Here the first place will naturally be given to the 'Christian Year.' As the author states in the preface, it is a series of compositions adapted with more or less propriety to the successive portions of the Prayer-Book, whose leading principle it is intended to illustrate—viz., 'the importance of a sound rule of faith and of a sober standard of feeling in matters of practical religion.' Although the writer himself had a very modest opinion of its merits, it is scarcely too much to say that this book has had more influence in the direction indicated in his words just quoted than any book of recent times, and it has perhaps had a wider circulation. Whether a man is High Church or Low Church, or no Church at all, he generally possesses a copy of the 'Christian Year'; many devout people make a pocket-companion of it, and read or learn the hymns as they occur at the Church seasons. As I have already said, Keble owed the general idea and the title to Bishop Ken's collection. It is a curious sort of coincidence that the only hymns of Ken's which have survived the oblivion of the rest of his book are those for morning and evening. These are in almost every hymnal to this day, and very near them will be found Keble's morning and evening hymns.

The 'Lyra Innocentium' is decidedly a book to read. It has rather gone out of fashion, partly as following the inevitable fate of *all* books, which, unless their overwhelming merit makes them classical, find their way to the upper shelves of one's bookcase after a few years of popularity. The 'Lyra Innocentium' is inferior on the whole to the 'Christian Year.' But the neglect into which it has fallen is partly due to a misconception of its contents. Whereas the verses are supposed to be *for* children, they are really *about* children, and are meant for the edification of grown-up people. We also owe to the movement the 'Lyra Apostolica' from its poetical supporters, the 'Baptistery' by Isaac Williams, and Newman's 'Verses on Various Occasions.'

I do not want to claim for the movement more than its due; but there cannot be any doubt that we owe several excellent collections of hymns to the stimulating influence of its poetical writers—*e.g.*, the charming 'Lyra Germanica' by Miss Winkworth, the 'Lyra Anglicana' collected by the Rev. R. H. Baynes, and any number of other collections from the Catholic and other schools.

The fact is, the Oxford poets felt a great want in English hymnology, and did a good deal to supply it, and others have followed their example on different theological lines. The result is that the 'Christian Year' marks a distinct epoch in the history of English hymns. Before 1830 they were little better than metrical versions of the Psalms, redeemed, of course, by some beautiful hymns of a subjective kind by such writers as Cowper, Newton, Toplady, and the Wesleys. The change consequent on the Catholic Revival is very striking; and if we compare such a collection as 'Ancient and Modern' with the most popular hymnal before its time—say, the 'Mitre'—we shall see the difference in the large number of first-rate new English hymns, besides translations from the Greek, Latin, and German, which have been added to our store.

When I was a small choir-boy the 'Hymnal Noted' was brought out by the Rev. Thomas Helmore. It was distinctly on the lines of the Catholic movement, and was, of course, only used in what we should call the most 'advanced' churches. It consisted of translations from the Latin office-hymns, almost entirely the work of Dr. Neale, set to the ancient melodies, with more or less suitability, by Mr. Helmore. Our first reformers had regretted the loss of these fine old hymns, which they were obliged to forego in the absence of adequate translators. This book was an attempt at realizing their wishes. It has almost entirely ceased to be used as a collection,* though many of its separate hymns have been incorporated into 'Hymns Ancient and Modern.' The old hymns thus preserved

---

* It is still used for the office hymns at St. Alban's, Holborn; St. Barnabas, Pimlico, and a few other churches; but even there it is supplemented by more modern collections—*e.g.*, the 'People's Hymnal,' or 'Ancient and Modern.'

have been altered (some regard them as improved, others as spoilt) to bring them up (or down) to modern taste. The fact is, the 'Hymnal Noted,' like certain other things which owed their birth to the revival, has been found too mediæval for the present day, and was bound to die a natural death, under the modern reaction against the mediævalism of the earlier Tractarians. But it did good in introducing a more objective style of hymn into our public worship. And while this book has died out of use, its place has been taken by 'Ancient and Modern,' which aims at meeting the old and new taste from all sorts of sources. The success of this collection, which was first brought out in 1861, has been quite phenomenal. On the one hand, as was to be expected, it raised a storm of opposition to the doctrines involved;* on the other hand, it called forth several important works on hymnology, various collections of sacred lyrics for private use, about fifty supplements to, and new editions of, books in common use, and about a hundred entirely new collections. It is true that all this might have come about independently of the Catholic Revival. Those who think otherwise naturally point to the elevated doctrinal tone of the religious poetry since written, and also to many distinguished new hymn-writers of the Catholic school, as establishing the connection between the poetical and the religious revival.

It is worth a passing remark that a corresponding want has been felt, and a similar influence has been at work to remedy it, outside the English Church. Father Faber, the eloquent convert from the Anglican Communion, wrote a collection of hymns for use at the Brompton Oratory, from which the general favourites, 'The Pilgrims of the Night' and 'O Paradise!' are taken. While the English Church had no office-hymns worth mentioning, the Romanists had

* Dr. Colenso, for instance, condemned it in strong terms on the ground of the worship which it involved, or implied, to Jesus Christ, whose equality in the Godhead he disputed.

nothing *but* office-hymns; and, as Father Faber tells us, it was no uncommon thing to find a devout Romanist poring over the pages of John and Charles Wesley in search of something which his own Church had not provided. Curiously enough, while the English Church wanted *objective* hymns, the Roman wanted the *subjective*. Both have been supplied to some extent with what they wanted, and I think both are indebted to the same religious movement for the realization of their want, and for what has been done to meet it. Before leaving the subject of hymns I ought not to forget the beautiful 'Hymns for Children,' by Mrs. C. F. Alexander, or the numerous Christmas and Easter carols, which are undoubtedly fruits of the Catholic Revival.

There was one branch of literature which the Oxford writers almost entirely neglected, and that was Biblical criticism. Dr. Pusey's works on the 'Minor Prophets' and his exposition of the Book of Daniel are the solitary exceptions. Mozley says with great candour: They set forth 'no original views of duty, and not much to meet the great problems of the age, though a good deal to impede their solution. With regard to absence of Biblical criticism, it is best to state the facts, and leave them to themselves. There was hardly such a thing as Biblical criticism in this country at the beginning of this century. Poole's Synopsis contained all that an ordinary clergyman could wish to know. Arnold is described as in all his glory at Rugby, with Poole's Synopsis on one side and Facciolati on the other. *He* knew the value of the book; but at that very time, if a country clergyman chanced to find that he had *two* copies of the work, and therefore had one to spare, he would have found it difficult to obtain five shillings for the five volumes.'*

People differ very much about the translations of the Fathers undertaken by the Oxford writers. Some put them

* 'Reminiscences.'

almost on a level with Holy Scripture; others regard them as useless lumber, or, at all events, think that the precious jewels they contain are so rare and far apart that life is too short to search for them. These people ought to be the first to give the meed of praise to any set of men who were ready to sacrifice days and nights to the mastery of the patristic Greek and Latin, and to the still harder task of rendering them into facile and attractive English. Whatever the practical and permanent results of their labours, they undoubtedly stirred up a taste in this venerable field of theology. Besides the editions sent forth from Oxford and Cambridge, there were numerous publications by private translators, who preferred to work independently to being hampered with the restrictions of a series. And the revival of taste extended to collectors, who used to ransack the second-hand bookstalls in search of Augustines and Chrysostoms, with the result that prices went up considerably. Mozley tells us that those who acquired old copies about this time will often find the old 7s. 6d. not quite rubbed out on the fly-leaf, and in its place substituted *five guineas.* Those who are disposed to speak flippantly of the Fathers may just be reminded that Macaulay was very fond of St. Chrysostom, and carried his huge tomes with him during a long foreign journey. Who shall say that he owes none of his attractions to the golden-mouthed?

There is one field of literature which owes a great deal to the Oxford Movement—viz., that devoted to the history, construction, and significance of the offices of the English Church as contained in the Book of Common Prayer. A stimulus was given to liturgical studies some years before the movement. Shepherd, a clergyman of much promise, had announced a Prayer-Book with historical illustrations, and was working at it vigorously when he died. The work, thus left in a fragmentary state, was eventually published by his daughter. That a very wide interest was felt in the subject was proved by the fact that the subscriptions amounted to several thousand pounds. This interest may have been chiefly of an antiquarian kind. Many a man who has got the money will spend thousands in illuminated missals and breviaries without being at all a Churchman. But the antiquary often paves the way for the theologian.

In 1832, a year before the appearance of the first 'Tract for the Times,' William Palmer brought out his 'Origines Liturgicæ,' than which, as Mozley observes, 'there is not a more interesting work to a scholar and divine, and hardly a more useful one to an ordinary clergyman.' Dean Church speaks of it as 'by far the best book in the English language on the subject.'

This work, and others that followed it, were more than mere researches into antiquity. They were devotional, and had a distinctly doctrinal, in addition to an historical, object. They were intended to show, and did show very effectively, that the outward forms and ritual of the English Church were inseparably interwoven with its teaching, and that both had descended to it from the earliest ages of Christianity. Especially valuable in this direction also are the works of another writer of the same school, the Rev. John Mason Neale, whose translations of the liturgies of SS. Basil and Chrysostom and others have done so much to popularize this class of studies, and to make our own offices more interesting and intelligible. It was books of this kind which gave the impetus to liturgical study that has resulted in the many manuals we now possess on the Prayer-Book. With the exception of Wheatly's now somewhat obsolete work, there was very little in this way to be had before 1850. Now we have our Blunts, Procters, Maclears, Wordsworths, Harold Brownes, and Evan Daniels bringing out something fresh every year on every part of the Prayer-Book, from the Communion-office to the Thirty-nine Articles. And a revival, or, rather, an original spirit of inquiry, has been stirred up consequently in regard to all sorts of ancient and foreign liturgies, whether orthodox or so-called heretical. By a very easy transition the attention thus aroused has been turned to the serious literature in general of other Communions. Pascal, Massillon, Bourdaloue, Bossuet, representing the French Church; Luis de Granada, Antonio de Guevara, and other Spanish ecclesiastics have been translated and 'adapted' for English readers, who scarcely knew their names fifty years ago.

It is to this spirit of Catholic sympathy that we owe the translation of such works as Rosmini's 'Five Wounds of the Church,' introduced a few years ago to English readers by the late Canon Liddon. That revered name recalls a host of literary recollections of which the Canon's figure was the centre. As the disciple and exponent of Dr. Pusey, and at the same time the trusted friend and adviser of a younger generation, who began where the Oxford Movement left off, he formed a connecting-link between the older Tractarian school and its modern developments. His sermons and other precious works, while fully recognising the modern spirit of inquiry and healthy criticism, have had perhaps more weight than any other recent writings to keep this tendency within legitimate bounds. His name suggests many others eminent in the pulpit and in literature—fruits of the Revival certainly—but it will not be necessary to speak of men whom everyone can hear, or of books that are on every table.

There is a lighter literature of the movement that is worth mentioning, especially as it is passing out of the knowledge of the present generation of readers. I refer to the many little historical tales, chiefly published by Messrs. Parker and Joseph Masters. They illustrated striking periods and events in Church history. Dr. Neale, before mentioned as a liturgist, stands also in the front rank as a good teller of stories. Independently of the natural fate of all books not absolutely immortal, their drawback, under the altered conditions of Church thought and feeling at the present day, lies in the author's strong mediæval sympathies.

8

He was essentially a mediævalist and antiquary; and while his qualities of this kind permeate all his books, and give them a charm of their own for readers similarly minded, I think they prevented them from being read very extensively. Speaking for myself, I confess that as a boy I much preferred tales of English life and character to the most picturesque descriptions of saints, martyrs, and persecutions. If all boys are more or less alike, I can understand the neglect which has fallen on Dr. Neale's 'Lent Legends' and 'Tales of Christian Heroism;' but it might do some of us good to read them now as a corrective to the sensational taste of the present day. There were two other good story-tellers of one's youth that deserve a better fate. The Rev. William Gresley, Prebendary of Lichfield, gave us the 'Siege of Lichfield,' a tale of the bloody conflict between Cavaliers and Roundheads; 'The Forest of Arden,' a tale of the Reformation; and 'Coniston Hall,' a tale of the Revolution of 1688.

And the Rev. F. E. Paget, Rector of Elford, gave us such favourites as 'Tales of the Village' and 'Tales of the Village Children.' Each of these wrote plenty more—sermons, essays, moral counsels, magazine articles, etc., all on the lines of the movement. They were extremely sensible works, and would strike us now as wonderfully moderate; but in their day they were regarded as among the subtle devices of the enemy to mislead the young and innocent.

I must not forget the pretty allegories by the Rev. Edward Monro—*e.g.*, 'The Combatants,' 'The Journey Home,' 'The Vast Army,' etc.—all well-written, but liable to two defects, which, as I am bound to be impartial, I may as well mention. First, it must be confessed they were rather feeble by the side of the immortal 'Pilgrim's Progress' of John Bunyan, which has spoilt people for all other religious allegories. Macaulay was amusingly severe on such imitations. I give his remarks below.*

* 'The peculiar glory of Bunyan is that those who most hated his doctrines have tried to borrow the help of his genius. A Catholic version

Another writer of allegories, to whom the same criticism applies, was the Rev. W. Adams. The second defect under which they both laboured was a species of false sentiment which pervaded their little books like the odour of faded flowers. This quality was even more conspicuous in certain pretty domestic tales which came out at about the same time. In the allegories, of course, one was prepared for an idealism and exaltation of character which would appear forced and unnatural in a description of actual life. Even to my juvenile sense 'Harry and Archie, or the First and Last Communion' (Monro) created a feeling of nausea from its general air of unreality, and it was just this quality which prevented boys of my age from enjoying such very good stories, in spite of their attractions otherwise.

Whatever Dr. Neale's peculiarities were, there was no want of robustness about him. His ideas were too ascetic,

---

of his parable may be seen with the head of the Virgin in the title-page. On the other hand, those Antinomians for whom his Calvinism is not strong enough may study the pilgrimage of Hephzibah, in which nothing will be found which can be construed into an admission of free agency and universal redemption. But the most extraordinary of all the acts of vandalism by which a fine work of art was ever defaced was committed so late as the year 1853. It was determined to transform the "Pilgrim's Progress" into a Tractarian book. The task was not easy, for it was necessary to make the two Sacraments the most prominent objects in the allegory; and of all Christian theologians, avowed Quakers excepted, Bunyan was the one in whose system the Sacraments held the least prominent place. However, the Wicket-gate became a type of Baptism, and the House Beautiful of the Eucharist. The effect of this change is such as surely the ingenious person who made it never contemplated; for as not a single pilgrim passes through the Wicket-gate in infancy, and as Faithful hurries past the House Beautiful without stopping, the lesson which the fable in its altered shape teaches is, that none but adults ought to be baptized, and that the Eucharist may safely be neglected. Nobody would have discovered from the original "Pilgrim's Progress" that the author was not a Pædobaptist. To turn his book into a book against pædobaptism was an achievement reserved for an Anglo-Catholic divine.'—(Article on John Bunyan in the *Encyclopædia Britannica*.)

and he had too great an abhorrence of all the ways of Dissenters (whose stories for children were then specially sentimental) to be a sentimentalist himself. To compare small things with great—there was the same sort of difference between him and some of his compeers as adult readers notice between Thackeray and Dickens. The pathos of the former makes one feel an awkward sensation about the throat, or inclined to wipe one's spectacles, because it is perfectly real and natural. There was a rugged and masculine grandeur about some of Neale's translated hymns, together with an antique freedom of expression, which has been softened down (some think to their detriment) by modern editors. But where pathos was inevitable, Dr. Neale could be very affecting—the more so, of course, because he was true to nature.*

Of all the writers of fiction on the side of the Catholic Revival the most voluminous and the most widely read is Miss C. M. Yonge. Like her friend John Keble, she set apart a large portion of her profits for religious objects. 'The Heir of Redclyffe,' for instance, went to fit out the missionary schooner *Southern Cross* for Bishop Selwyn; and the proceeds of 'The Daisy Chain' were devoted to the building of a missionary college at Auckland, New Zealand.

I remember that about the time of Confirmation some senior friends kindly lent me 'The Heir of Redclyffe,' then

---

* On the first point, compare his original translation of the 'Urbs Beata' as written for the 'Hymnal Noted,' *e.g.*,

> 'From celestial realms descending,
>   Ready for the nuptial bed,
> To His presence, deck'd with jewels,
>   By her Lord shall she be led:
> All her streets, and all her bulwarks,
>   Of pure gold are fashioned'—

with the version in 'Ancient and Modern.'

The second point is well illustrated in the 'Stichera of the Last Kiss,' from his 'Hymns of the Eastern Church,' which are very touching.

a new book, in hopes of making it a vehicle for religious instruction. But I was much more interested in 'Oliver Twist,' 'Uncle Tom's Cabin,' and the weekly instalments of 'Woman and her Master' in the *London Journal*; and when my good friends asked me how I liked such and such incidents, I am afraid I had too much respect for their feelings to be strictly veracious, for I found that excellent book extremely dry and tedious.

A very striking feature of the period was the large number of tales for choristers which came out during the height of the Oxford Movement and for some years afterwards. The following are just a few from an old publisher's list.

'The Chorister Brothers,' 'The Children of the Chapel,' 'In the Choir and out of the Choir,' 'The Island Choir, or, The Children of the Child Jesus;' 'The Two Surplices,' 'The Chorister's Fall,' 'The Choristers of St. Mary's,' 'Little Walter the Lame Chorister,' 'Michael the Chorister,' 'The Singers,' 'The Little Choristers, or, Is it Fair?'

Some of these excellent little books were open to the same objection as the sacred allegories and the other stories I have just mentioned, that is in a certain unreality there was about them. The mischievous and precocious little imp with whom we are all familiar can hardly be described as a devout chorister, in spite of his angelic face and white surplice: as a rule he is not given to religious exercises, nor does he languish and die early. And a further objection which might be urged against these tales, from a literary point of view, was that they were written 'for a purpose.' One hates books written for a purpose, as a rule, but in this case I think it justifies them.

In my first lecture I mentioned the laxity and irreverence of choirs in the days preceding the Oxford Movement, or before there had been time for its effects to be at all general. I referred specially to cathedral choirs; but even in ordinary churches there was sad need for a reformation. As a remedy there were two points which the Catholic revivalists aimed at, first, to infuse a religious tone into choristers; and, secondly, to vest them in surplices. The surplice had the outward advantage of an appropriate uniform, besides being a reminder to him who wore it of the spirit in which his work ought to be done.

The inculcation of these ideas was the 'purpose' of the tales for choristers which came out in shoals while there was any demand for them. The use of the surplice and cassock (I think the second was a little later in general adoption) was, of course, advocated in more serious books; but the advantage of these vestments was kept well to the front in the stories, and I doubt whether any of the heavier arguments which were employed have done so much to make them popular. Now that surpliced choirs are so general, it is hard to conceive the prejudice which waited on their introduction. The unpretentious little tales I have mentioned did their share towards removing this prejudice, and (what is more important) in helping to raise the tone of choristers in character and behaviour. In churches where the surplice was introduced there was a marked improvement in the men and boys, and a good deal more supervision over their musical and religious training than had hitherto been bestowed. It became almost a *sine qua non* that the adult chorister should be a communicant, and not merely a man with a voice; and the choir-boys were well looked after by the clergy—almost always prepared for Confirmation, and that at an earlier age than had been the rule. The result was manifest in the persons themselves, and in the way they rendered divine service.

Now that musical services and surpliced choirs are the rule, it is to be feared that we are in danger of the usual penalty of success—in other words, that the standard aimed at among choristers and their trainers is not so high, at all events in a religious sense, as it was when the surplice was looked upon as a rag of Popery. But besides tales, there were numerous books of devotion for choristers. Perhaps the most celebrated was one called 'The Devout Chorister,' consisting of thoughts on his vocation, and a manual of prayers for his use, by Thomas Frederick Smith, Fellow of Magdalene. The copy I have was given to me by an old friend who had joined the Roman Church with his mother, and in turning out his old Anglican books, he presented me with that and some others which he thought I should take care of. The author makes a suggestion in the preface which is perhaps as appropriate to-day as it was in 1848.*

There were any number of books of devotion for the general public, some excellent, some, as was to be expected at a time of religious fervour, going just a little beyond the bounds of common-sense. 'The Manual,' for instance (by the Rev. W. E. Heygate), which its title-page describes as 'chiefly intended for the poor,' gives some advice on reading which we should now think rather childish.

'A poor man has not much time for reading, and therefore it is necessary to spend that little well: neither is he the best judge of what is true or false, or of what is good or bad for him. The poor, therefore, should never buy the tracts and cheap prints and songs which are hawked about. One half of them is bad, and the other half useless. Nor should the poor man read newspapers, which will only trouble and deceive him, unless there is some great news,

* 'It is also much to be desired that some kind of cœnobium or college should be founded in the precincts of our cathedral and collegiate churches, for the education and training of such choristers who may be willing to devote their after-life to the service of the Church, either as lay teachers or in Holy Orders. The absence of some provision of this kind for choristers, some means of retaining them for ecclesiastical employments, where a right disposition is not wanting on their own part, must be painfully felt in many ways; for it seems not only injurious to them, but a reflection on the Church's maternal care, that they who have dedicated the first-fruits of their years and strength to the special service of her courts, should be turned adrift at a most critical period of life, for no other reason than because their voice breaks down, or their minstrelsy becomes exhausted.'

like a battle, or a shipwreck, or a fire. . . . The poor man's books are his Bible and Prayer-Book, and *this book*, and, if he can get them, Nelson's " Fasts and Festivals," " The Imitation of Christ," and such others as the clergyman of the parish may lend or give.'

Some years ago an intelligent British workman spotted the passage, and wrote to Mr. Gladstone, as in some way identified with the religious party who had been guilty of circulating such 'pernicious trash,' to ask him what he thought of it. Mr. Gladstone replied that he had never heard of the book, and that the advice must be taken *cum grano* as the opinion of one man, who was alone responsible for it.

It would take too long to mention the scores of 'Little Prayer-Books,' 'Altar Manuals,' 'Meditations,' etc., which belong to the movement. Whether they all belong to literature is a question. Many of them were too exotic in character to be permanent favourites with Anglicans; others, however, being compiled from the best English and foreign theologians, did a great deal to raise the devotional taste here. In fact, they did much to create it. Two of the most deservedly popular books of this kind, both thoroughly English in their character, were 'Steps to the Altar,' by Mr. Scudamore, and 'Eucharistica.' The latter was anonymously compiled, but issued with an introduction by Samuel Wilberforce, then Bishop of Oxford. It consists entirely of prayers and readings from the great English divines from Hooker to Bishop Wilson—and, I believe, may still be had in new editions. Many others have gone the way of all books, for even here the influence of fashion is felt, and what pleased one generation is forgotten by the next.

It will be seen at once that I have only just touched the fringe of a very wide subject. I have mentioned some of the leading authors, favouring or distinctly supporting the Catholic Revival, and have said a little about some of their best-known books. I have also mentioned some inferior men and some inferior books, in a literary sense, which nevertheless have had a good deal of influence collectively in the same direction.

To deal with the subject exhaustively would be the work of a life-time, for I do not think there has ever been a movement, secular or religious, which has involved so much writing. Indeed its already voluminous collection is being added to largely every year.

Almost every species of composition on which I have touched as emanating from the Catholic side has led to writings of different schools, either to modify what their authors considered an inaccurate theology, or emphatically to contradict it, or to meet the wants of their own disciples, or haply to express the views of thinkers who differed from everybody else in the world.

In conclusion, allow me to say, what probably is too well known to need saying at all, that in whatever other way the reign of our gracious Queen is distinguished, one of its leading characteristics will be its wonderful literature— exceeding even that of Queen Elizabeth and of Queen Anne put together — and one of its most valuable parts will be the literature of the Catholic Revival.

As in other cases where a literature is so extensive in bulk and range of subjects, there will, of course, be a great deal of rubbish that will go to line the inside of trunks or to wrap up small purchases of grocery; but, while this disappears, the really solid part will remain a treasure to our Church as long as her services are conducted and her sermons preached in the English language.

LECTURE VI.

SOME FRUITS OF THE CATHOLIC REVIVAL.

QUITE lately I heard our esteemed rector preach a sermon without a text. I am now going to reverse the process by giving you a text without a sermon. My remarks will not be of that serious and dignified nature to entitle them to be called a sermon, but as a peg to hang my remarks upon, I will borrow a text from the Rev. Daniel Wilson's 'Appeal to Evangelicals' (1850), from which I have already made one or two quotations. He says:

'No efforts have been omitted by the opposite party to imbue the Church at large with their novel views. Music, painting, poetry, architecture, eloquent appeals to the feelings, tales for the young, parables, similitudes, every species of attraction that ingenuity could invent, or refined taste suggest, has been put in requisition. All classes of society have been assailed. The press has been largely tampered with. Our public institutions have been made the vehicle of proselytism. The plague has spread to our colonial possessions, and exhibits itself there in a form still more open and undisguised than at home.'

As early as 1835, Mr. Newman issued a pamphlet recommending the restoration of suffragan bishops as a means of effecting a more equal distribution of episcopal duties. It would be unfair to claim for the Oxford Movement all the credit of the increase in the episcopate which has come about since that date, but it is interesting to see its leader advocating the very means which have since been adopted, and calling attention to the very Act of Parliament (26 Henry VIII., c. 14) on whose authority the suffragan bishops have been appointed, as sufficient for the purpose, without involving organic changes. If the increase in the episcopate is not altogether due to the movement, it is at least due to that religious activity to which the movement itself owes its birth, and which the movement in return has done very much to help forward. At the beginning of the eighteenth century there were not so many people in the whole of England and Wales as there are now in the London postal district. The country was then divided into twenty-six dioceses, the population and revenues of which varied so greatly that in 1831 a Royal Commission was appointed to inquire into the whole matter of Episcopal income and patronage. The result of the deliberations of this Commission was a proposal that, for greater efficiency of administration, the bishops' incomes should be equalized to a considerable extent, and the area of the dioceses rearranged: but it was *not* proposed to increase the number of bishops. It was in accordance with this programme, and in consequence of some popular proceedings in the particular case, that the Commissioners obtained the suppression of the see of Bristol. In 1836 its territory was divided among the dioceses of Gloucester, Salisbury, and Bath and Wells, the title and cathedral falling to the see of Gloucester, which had the name of Bristol attached to it.

Simultaneously with this partition of the see of Bristol, and aided by its revenues, the new diocese of Ripon was created for half Yorkshire. But the rapid growth of the Northern and Midland towns made the creation of fresh bishoprics imperative, a mere redistribution of those already in existence being insufficient for the wants of the increased population, and the localities in which the increase had chiefly taken place. The result has been the creation of the new dioceses of Manchester, St. Albans, Liverpool, Newcastle, Southwell, and Wakefield; while in the South of England an ancient diocese in Cornwall has been revived, and an Act of Parliament has recently been obtained to restore that of Bristol, which ought never to have been suppressed; and, as the required endowment has been obtained, a bishop will no doubt soon be appointed. We thus see that the twenty-six dioceses have been increased to thirty-two, presided over by as many bishops, in addition to the Archbishops of Canterbury and York. But it was not till 1870 that Newman's special suggestion was realized by the restoration of the long dormant class of suffragan bishops. Their number is now seventeen; and it is scarcely necessary to say that they form a considerable factor in the home episcopate. It is interesting to notice, in passing, that during the consecration of Dr. Mackenzie, the first of these suffragan bishops, the Greek Archbishop of Syra and Tenos happened to be staying in England, and took part in the ceremony, an act of intercourse between East and West which is full of significance.

The development of the colonial episcopate has been going on simultaneously. Though initiated in 1787, it had numbered no more than five sees down to 1836; but in 1841 a fund for its increase was inaugurated, and the work has since been going on rapidly. In this sense, if in no other, 'the plague has spread to our colonial possessions.'

Here are signs of life which it is impossible to ignore, and no one but a bitter partisan will deny that the restoration of that life is to a great extent due to the Oxford Movement. Sixty years ago the fortunes of the Church of England had sunk to the lowest ebb; hope was all but extinguished; the Church's days seemed numbered. Few men now living have before them the condition of the Church as it was at that time; and yet to appreciate rightly what she is *now* it is necessary to recall what she was *then*. As I said in my first lecture, the antagonistic feeling was summed up in 1834 by Lord Ripon introducing his Bill into Parliament for the suspension of the legislative and judicial functions of the bishops. The Bill did not pass, but that such a proposal should have been seriously entertained speaks volumes for the political and religious conditions under which it was brought forward. These conditions are vividly and accurately described by the Rev. William Palmer in his 'Narrative of Events connected with the Publication of the Tracts for the Times,' and also in an article written by him for the *Contemporary Review* in May, 1883:

'The press groaned beneath the perpetual issue of pamphlets, treatises, discourses—all bent on the reformation and correction of the Church from head to foot. To open one of these disquisitions—which undertook at a week's notice to present a spick-and-span new creation, in which imperfection was to be unknown—you might suppose that the Church of England was a mass of corruption, folly, and bigotry. Everything was wrong, and required a radical change. Nothing could be hoped for, except after the expulsion of bishops from the House of Lords, the overthrow of chapters, the abolition of religion in the Universities, the radical reform of the worship and the doctrine of the Church in a liberal direction. The Prayer-Book was to be divested of its antique rubbish, swept clean of the supernaturalism which had descended to it from the Middle Ages, relieved of those continual professions of belief in the Trinity, the deity of Christ, the belief in Divine providence, and other points which so greatly troubled the delicate consciences of those Christians who were anxious to fraternize with Unitarianism and Infidelity. The Church of England of the future was to become a congeries of sects at utter variance with each other in doctrine and discipline, each preserving its distinctive peculiarities, with the single exception of the present Church of England, which, by authority of Parliament, and without any reference to the wishes of its bishops, clergy, or people, was to be arbitrarily remodelled and vitally changed.*

'Such was the disorganization of the public mind that Dr. Arnold of Rugby ventured to propose that all denominations should be united by Act of Parliament with the Church of England, on the principle of retaining all their distinctive errors and absurdities.'†

'What claims special notice in all these proposed changes was the spirit of irreverence which was widely characteristic of the period, together with the prevailing want of principle. All who have written on the events of that time have noticed the extreme and dangerous unsettlement of opinion which manifested itself about the year 1830, the era when the reform mania was at its height, and when " reform " was decided to be the panacea for every human ill. In the midst of this revolutionary turmoil the Church and Christianity were in danger of being swept from their old foundations, and replaced upon the philosophic basis of the nineteenth century.'‡

On comparing the Church of England then with what she is now, one is inclined to say with Shakespeare, 'Look here upon this picture and on *this*.' But more important than any increase in *numbers* has been the increase in fervour and activity on the part of individual bishops, which has never been more marked at any period of the Church's history than during the years succeeding the Oxford Movement. To this, I think, we are largely indebted to the influence and example of that single prelate who was appointed to the See of Oxford at the critical period of 1845—I refer, of course, to Samuel Wilberforce. It had been the custom for speakers on public platforms, when alluding to our episcopal overseers, to compare them to certain useful but immovable

---

* Palmer, in the *Contemporary Review*.
† Palmer's narrative.
‡ *Ibid*. Quoted by Dean Burgon in his 'Life of Hugh James Rose.'

pieces of timber used to support the metals on railroads, and technically known as *sleepers;* or, to put it in the more polite language of Dean Burgon, 'the popular notion of a bishop's office before his (Wilberforce's) time was connected above all things with images of dignified leisure and serene isolation.'

'Should it ever come to be inquired hereafter,' the Dean continues, 'Wherein does Wilberforce's claim to the Church's gratitude chiefly consist? the answer ought not to be far to seek. He imparted a new character to the work of an English bishop; left on the entire episcopate the abiding impress of his own earnest spirit and extraordinary genius. Ever since Samuel Wilberforce was appointed to the See of Oxford the office of a bishop has been identified with nothing so much as incessant labour, ubiquitous exertion, the utmost publicity. Wilberforce set before himself the necessity of restoring to full efficiency the ancient mechanism of the diocese. Thus his rural deans were not only taught to hold chapters, and to submit for discussion questions of the day to the clergy of their respective rural deaneries, reporting the result to the Bishop, but they were periodically invited to Cuddesdon for deliberation with their chief. In this way were first set on foot those many diocesan associations, which, under his personal guidance, were in the end brought to a state of the highest efficiency. Countless were the schemes he originated for stimulating the religious life of his diocese, as by local conferences, by gatherings of the clergy and laity, by public meetings held for Church purposes, etc.'*

The Dean adds a very interesting account of Wilberforce's work in the conduct of *missions*, and in inaugurating those special *Lenten courses of sermons* which have since grown into an institution. Both these departments of Church work may be said to owe their life to the Bishop who had the courage to suggest or guide them at a time

* Burgon on Samuel Wilberforce.

when such agencies were sorely needed, but when any indiscretion in their conduct would have been fatal to their continuance. And besides originating new works, we owe to him the infusion of fresh life and character into the mode of administering ordinations and confirmations, which from dry and formal ceremonies he changed into such impressive services as could never be forgotten by those who were present. This was largely owing to the strong personality of him who presided over them, and to the personal interest which he took in each individual candidate, as well as to those wonderful addresses in which he turned to account the passing incidents of the moment as types and parables for the conveyance of his teaching. If he did not originate, he at least made a great deal more of the confirmation addresses than had ever been done before.

I had the pleasure of hearing him on more than one occasion, but the last has become peculiarly impressive from the circumstance that it was only a few days before he met with the accident which caused his death. It was during the summer of 1873 that he administered the rite of confirmation at St. Peter's Church, Vauxhall, and I believe he never administered it again anywhere. His biographer's description of his general mode of administration would here be peculiarly appropriate.

'Sympathy with the young was a marked feature in his character, and he felt intensely the possibilities for good which were before the young people presented to him. Then, it was one of Bishop Wilberforce's peculiar gifts that, when he did thus realize anything very deeply, his whole bearing, voice and gesture—aye, and countenance—were, if such an expression may be permitted, transfigured by the thought or feeling which possessed him; so that the living man as he stood before you was, almost without words, the expression of that feeling. When, in addition to all this, his power of language is remembered, the energy and deep feeling which was apparent in every sentence and every tone, together with his charm of voice and special fertility and variety of phrase, no one will be surprised at the prodigious impression which his confirmations always made alike upon the young and upon the old.'*

It should also be mentioned that we owe the restoration of the Church Convocations, which, as I have already stated, had been dormant for about one hundred and fifty years, to him more than to any other single man. In the institution, too, of Cuddesdon Training College, the clergy have a continual reminder of their obligations to this distinguished prelate. It will be remembered that he was transferred from the Deanery of Westminster to the Bishopric of Oxford in October, 1845, on the eve of Newman's secession, and when we consider that his administration of the diocese extended over one of the most critical periods in the history of the Church of England—including as it did the troublous days of the Hampden controversy, the Gorham judgment, the publication of 'Essays and Reviews,' the 'higher criticism,' of Dr. Colenso, to say nothing of the special difficulties consequent on the Oxford Movement—we shall perhaps be inclined to see a special Providence in the appointment of such a man to such a place. He has been called the 'remodeller of the episcopate.' Certainly the episcopate has put on a new character under his influence and example. It is satisfactory that its renewed life and energy are not confined to any particular school in the Church, but I suppose no one will deny that they have been most fully exhibited in that school which we identify with the Catholic Revival, and to which, after all, Bishop Wilberforce belonged more than to any other. That he was unable to follow it into all its developments is not to say that he was not with it in leading principles. These, and the simple practices which they involved, were met with even more violent opposition in their day than the

* Life.

more imposing manifestations of doctrine and ritual which have followed in later stages of the revival.

Wilberforce used to say that he belonged to no school or party—possibly in the sense that the Catholic Church is neither one nor the other—but the preachers he gathered round him for the Lenten and Mission Sermons before mentioned, though widely selected, included many names of such marked Churchmanship as an opponent of the revival would certainly not have included, at a time when prejudice was high against them. Moberly, Wordsworth, Magee, Milman, Alford, Goulburn, Butler, Pusey, Liddon, Benson, Randall, Carter, Evans and Skinner, are a few who in their turn have become fresh centres of activity to carry on the Church's work, certainly not on the lines of ultra-Protestantism.

The change that has taken place in the number and character of the chief pastors of the Church is at least equalled by the improvement in the inferior clergy. Whatever we may think about the incompetence or indolence of particular men, there surely never was a time when the clergy as a body have exhibited more knowledge and industry, and more of that earnest and religious spirit which is likely to make their work a success, than at the present day.

I am far from saying that it is High Churchmen or Ritualists alone to whom this remark applies. One ought to be glad to acknowledge the good qualities of men of all schools; but if the improvement is due to anything, it is surely due in great measure to that high view of the ministerial office insisted on by the Tract writers, to that doctrine of sacerdotalism for which they were abused, and which, according to the interpretation put upon it, may become either one of the most powerful instruments for good, or the greatest means of corruption within the Church. From the Erastianism which regarded the clergyman as nothing more than a state-paid agent for the discharge of certain duties, and the delivery of certain lectures, little spiritual good was to be expected. This certainly was the popular idea of a minister before the revival; but it has since been made perfectly clear that ordination carries with it certain special graces and special responsibilities.

In Newman's expressive language, a man feels now that he can hardly expect to undertake the sacred office 'without being sprinkled with the blood of other souls.' In other words, a clergyman has not only to preach sermons, and perform marriages and burials, or even to be a benevolent and agreeable gentleman, but to administer the sacraments, of which he is the custodian, and to be all that is comprehended in the word 'Priest.'

It is interesting to notice, in passing, the general prejudice which used to attach to that word, as well as the word 'Catholic,' till quite recently. Both perfectly innocent words in themselves, they have had an exaggerated meaning infused into them (not altogether unreasonably) so that people became quite frightened at them. Their legitimate place in the vocabulary of the English Churchman is a fruit of the revival.

But the renewal of zeal has by no means been confined to the clergy. The desire to lead a higher kind of life, and to do some special work for the Church, resulting from the Anglo-Catholic teaching, has shown itself in a very striking manner in the establishment of those numerous societies for men and for women within the Church, which are among the phenomena of the age. I think the oldest of these societies is the 'Guild of the Holy Trinity,' founded at Oxford in 1844. Cambridge and Durham Universities have followed this example by the foundation of similar Guilds, with the same hallowed dedication, the former in 1857, the latter not till 1885. Besides these we have

    The Guild of St. Luke (1864) for the medical profession;
    The Guild of the Holy Standard for the army; and
    The Guild of the Holy Cross (1872) for the railway service.

One of the oldest and best known of these societies is the Guild of St. Alban, called after the British protomartyr, which has branches at various places in London and the country, and even in the colonies. This was started in the year of the great Exhibition (1851), and at the most unlikely place of Birmingham. It has done a splendid work in its time; but its members regret that it does not go on increasing. The great reason ought to be satisfactory, viz., that nearly every parish has its own particular societies, and there is therefore less inducement to join an outside institution than when it was the only outlet for zeal in that direction. The fact is that the desire for such organizations is so general, and their usefulness so fully recognised, that one finds them locally established everywhere, whether called by the name of 'guild,' 'society,' 'association,' or what not. If I was giving a paper on Guilds, I might be disposed to say something against them, for, of course, they have their dangers. All I say now is that all schools of Churchmen—High, Low, and Broad—have adopted them, and they are almost a *sine qua non* in a well-ordered parish.

Even the mediæval idea of life in community, and the stricter discipline which a common residence and perpetual obedience involve, is not unknown, and is favourably regarded in high ecclesiastical quarters. Among *men*, however, it cannot be said to have succeeded. *Sisterhoods*, on the other hand, have become a very popular institution. I think a great deal of the prejudice against this species of devotion was removed by the splendid work done by Florence Nightingale (herself not a sister) in the Crimea, under whom some of the members of the sisterhood founded by Dr. Pusey in 1845 had worked. That particular sisterhood, the first in England, was broken up in 1855, after the Crimean war, and the members were dispersed to form the nucleus of other societies of the same kind. The Sisterhoods of St. Margaret, East Grinstead; St. Raphael's, Bristol; All Saints', Margaret Street; the

Sisters of the Church, Kilburn; the Sisterhoods of St. John the Baptist, Clewer; of St. Mary, Wantage; and of St. Peter, Horbury, near Wakefield; are a few of the most important of those communities which have sprung up throughout the country within half a century. The words 'brotherhood,' 'sisterhood,' and 'guild,' have gone through the same phases of dislike, suspicion, guarded acceptance and positive approval, as the other words just mentioned, and illustrate the course of Church thought on the particular subjects. Whether we approve or disapprove of those institutions, their existence is a palpable fact, and one that is certainly a fruit of the Catholic Revival. The date of their foundation, and the names of those under whose fostering care they have been developed, are sufficient to identify them with the school which has the glory of their invention, but the *principle* is more widely recognised; and it is interesting to notice among certain Nonconformists— *e.g.*, Wesleyans and Congregationalists—the formation of religious societies with titles, if not with objects, which those bodies would have looked upon with abhorrence thirty years ago.

I ought just to notice the humbler, but perhaps equally important, communicants' guilds which have been established, under one name or another, in many parishes, partly to do Church work, but specially to promote reverence for the Holy Eucharist and regular attendance at the celebrations. These, of course, vary very much in their character, from the advanced 'Confraternity of the Blessed Sacrament' to the ordinary mild Anglican society. Their varying character is a healthy sign, as showing that schools, in other respects very different, have a common regard for the great Christian mystery. If the Oxford writers had one object in view more than another, it surely was to revive the ancient reverence for the Sacraments as the appointed channels of grace. This object has been well answered in the vastly different ideas about Holy Communion which are held now as compared with 1845, and the enormous increase in the number of communicants. This can only be spoken of in a general way, for the subject is too sacred to be made a matter of statistics, to say nothing of the danger of estimating real religious progress by the mere criterion of numbers. But the outward and visible sign is surely some indication of the inward and spiritual grace. And it must be confessed that the churches where the greatest stress has been laid on this point, and where the most visible results have been obtained, have been also those where the outward ceremonial has been accompanied by a corresponding spirituality in life and instruction. The number of communicants at such leading churches as St. Barnabas, Pimlico; All Saints', Margaret Street; St. Alban's, Holborn; St. Augustine's, Kilburn; St. John the Divine, Vassall Road; and St. Agnes, Kennington Park, is astonishing, especially on the great festivals—*e.g.*, Easter, Whitsunday, or Christmas—when the communicants are equal to several ordinary congregations.

The mention of churches leads me to say something about a more material evidence of the revival, which would perhaps strike the mere gatherer of statistics as its most significant development. I refer to church architecture. The condition of England during the first quarter of this century reminds one of Constantinople in 330 A.D., when the first Christian emperor pitched upon it for his capital. In both cases there were plenty of ancient models, but profound ignorance of art, and scarcely anybody capable of restoring an old building or designing a new one. 'Repaired and beautified' was an inscription frequently found in old churches, but, considering the alterations indicated by these words, we should be inclined to look upon them as a falsehood. Where a new building was necessitated, the architectural taste of the day involved its erection in a style of barbarous ugliness. There was a church near Oxford, for instance, which Mozley mentions as resembling nothing so much in its general proportions as a 'boiled rabbit.' Another has been mentioned to me, the style of which was called 'Day and Martin,' from its external resemblance to one of that celebrated firm's bottles of blacking. A stranger, seeing its interior for the first time (I have the anecdote from a clergyman, and therefore it must be strictly true), remarked to the verger that, whatever else happened in that church, there would be no danger of idolatry, for it resembled nothing in heaven or earth, or in the waters under the earth.

In the early days of the revival self-denial was inculcated in various ways. Prayer, fasting, and almsgiving were taught as the keys to heaven. I am afraid there has been a falling off in these points of late years, necessarily so perhaps as regards the great body of church-goers, who can hardly be expected to come up to the level of a select few. With an extended popularity every movement is apt to lose some of its original fervour. Anyhow, the amounts given by individuals for church building in the early days would surprise us. It was not at all an unknown thing for people to deny themselves a Continental holiday, or even greater necessities, for the sake of contributing towards the erection of churches on the Catholic lines where they were felt to be wanted. The mere getting of money for the purpose was no great difficulty where people of means were so terribly in earnest. St. Barnabas, Pimlico, cost £30,000. All Saints', Margaret Street (built to perpetuate the Margaret Chapel, where such men as Mr. Gladstone and Mr. Hope-Scott used to attend), cost double that amount. This will illustrate what was going on here and there all over the country. All Saints', Clifton, can scarcely have cost less than St. Barnabas, and the beautiful church at Bôdelwyddan, near St. Asaph, built by the Dowager Lady Willoughby de Broke, is quoted at £35,000. Whether built by the generosity of a single person or by public subscription, churches of this kind rose up between 1840 and 1860, if not exactly 'like an exhalation,' at all events with sufficient rapidity to alarm ultra-Protestants at the spread of the Oxford teaching. The necessity for building seemed to generate a school of architects. It is with those days that we associate the names of Pugin, Butterfield, Street, Scott, and Pearson. It was a case of supply and demand. Gothic work was wanted, and such Gothic architects as these arose and built. It was characteristic of the movement that Gothic, and not the classical or Renaissance, was considered the most suitable style. It was to pre-Reformation times that the revivalists looked back, through their abhorrence of the iconoclastic destruction consequent on the Puritan supremacy, and the many beautiful specimens of Gothic art in England were naturally taken as models. The symbolism which this species of architecture contained in such abundance was, moreover, inseparably allied with Christian doctrine, which can scarcely be said of the Renaissance style. On the one hand, this may illustrate the thoroughly *English* nature of the revival; on the other hand, it must be confessed that the devotion to one style was pushed to a length which now strikes us as ridiculous. No beauty, no appropriateness, was seen in any other style. It became practically an article of the Oxford creed that unless a man believed in Gothic architecture (and Gregorian music) he could not be a good Churchman. I am told that one of the Mozleys (I forget which) had been heard to say, when his views had become more enlarged, that he remembered the time when he felt it quite impossible to say his prayers in a gallery.

The effect of this absurd doctrine was seen in two very striking ways. There was a tendency to make every little bit of a parish church like a cathedral, with its side chapels, separate altars, etc., which necessitated everything on such a small scale as to destroy the object of a church for a united congregation; and secondly, it was thought necessary, in undoing the churchwardens' repairs and beautifications of the last century, to go to the other extreme, and to put up Gothic chancels, Gothic reredoses, Gothic pulpits, and Gothic ornaments in every church which came under renovation. Consequently much really good Renaissance work was ruthlessly destroyed as unchristian, and a hybrid and incongruous mixture of styles which had no sort of agreement was the result. This was just one of those crazes which are apt to occur in every reactionary movement where zeal is apt to get the better of knowledge. Even in brand-new Gothic churches mistakes were made during the education of the school of architects to which I have referred.

We have got past these mistakes now. Gothic art has been thoroughly studied, and the exclusive devotion to it has been followed by an eclecticism which recognises beauty in every style. As illustrating the change, Mr. Pearson lately told a friend of mine that he was quite glad of the eclectic and really more Catholic taste which recent times had developed, as the exclusion of one style by another, or, rather, of all styles by one, was detrimental to real artistic progress.

The effect of the revival on ecclesiastical architecture is seen in the present almost perfect condition of our cathedrals, as contrasted with the picture of them which I drew in my first lecture, in the improvement in our great parish churches, and in the numerous beautiful new churches which have been set up throughout the length and breadth of the country to provide for our increasing population. The interesting return of Lord Hampton upon church-building for the period of thirty-four years—viz., from 1840 to 1874—shows that during that time a sum of £25,548,703 was raised for the building and restoration of cathedrals and churches. It is well known that this return was by no means complete; and it is estimated that if it could have been made so, it would have represented an annual expenditure of at least a million pounds sterling upon this branch of Church work. It may be interesting to supplement this statement by the fact that from 1882 to 1890 inclusive a total sum of nearly eleven millions was raised (exactly £10,918,811) for church building and restoration, endowment of benefices, parsonage-houses, and burial-grounds. The figures represent voluntary offerings alone, grants from the Ecclesiastical Commission and of other bodies holding Church property in trust being carefully excluded. The figures were supplied by the incumbents of the livings concerned, and may safely be taken as accurate.*

Facts like these prove that the Church of England is a living reality. I casually referred to music. Let me say a few more words about it. It is well known that in the Middle Ages, when Gothic architecture had attained its perfect development, music was in its infancy. At the time when the great cathedrals were built the science of harmony was unknown, and the music of the Church was necessarily the Gregorian plain-song. Thus it happened that by a very natural association of ideas the two things, which had merely

* 'It is in no spirit of boastfulness, but rather for the purpose of encouragement, that we give the following particulars as to the voluntary offerings of Church-people during the year 1892. It must be premised that we do not include grants from the Ecclesiastical Commissioners or Queen Anne's Bounty, neither individual offerings privately contributed to societies and institutions. We find that a sum of £1,153,693 was devoted to the building, restoration and furnishing of churches; to the enlargement of burial-grounds, £31,289; to the endowment of benefices, £161,505; and to the erection of parsonage houses, £94,611. The grand total under the head of Church work amounts to £1,441,098, towards which the four dioceses of Wales gave the handsome sum of £90,042. Under the head of elementary education we find that the amount spent by the Church was £923,304, apportioned as follows: £109,234 for the building and enlargement of schools and training colleges, and for the maintenance of the same, £814,070. The large amount collected for the schools argues a very keen interest in education on the part of Churchmen, coupled with considerable self-denial, and for this reason we have given the above figures, as also in the hope that many who have hitherto held back from the work will add their own to the splendid efforts of their fellow Churchmen.'—*The Church Times* for March 2, 1894.

an accidental connexion, were inseparably allied in the minds of the revivalists, and Gothic architecture and Gregorian music were held to be in their respective ways the only proper exponents of Catholic doctrine. Consequently Gregorian tones were introduced at most of the representative churches. Books were written on the theory and practice of plain-song, the libraries of England and the Continent were ransacked for ancient melodies, psalters and hymnals were arranged on the old models thus brought to light, associations were formed for popularizing the subject, and a great stimulus was given to it. This absurd identification of things which had no necessary connexion has given way with time, and there are very few churches now where an entirely Gregorian service obtains. Even at the special services of the Gregorian association at St. Paul's it has been found desirable to relieve the severity of the performance by something a little less archaic in the shape of a favourite hymn or anthem. There has, in short, been a reaction, and people have got to see the mistake of excluding the best German, Italian, or Anglican work from the service of religion. It was no uncommon thing in the early days of the revival to hear an advanced man speak of such and such a church as in a benighted condition because 'Anglicans' were still used there for the psalms. Now people are more eclectic, and can see beauties in every style. The same stages of thought have been gone through here, in fact, as in architecture. The severe and simple music of the Gregorian school had one great recommendation from a religious point of view, and that was that, as a rule, the congregation were able to take their share of the service, instead of simply listening to the choir. Now, it is to be feared that the reaction against the old severity is tending towards the exclusion of the *vox populi* in certain churches where elaborate masses are performed—very beautiful as works of art, but utterly impossible to be joined in by the average church-goer. And this state of things unfortunately occurs at some of those churches where a few years back this was the very objection urged against everything that was not Gregorian. Only a few months ago certain letters appeared in the *Church Times* from old worshippers at St. Alban's, Holborn, who resented the changes introduced there by a new organist or choirmaster as destroying the congregational character of the services. And this is not an isolated case.

It certainly would be a great pity if the distinctive feature of the Prayer-Book, as compared with the Roman Breviary and Missal, were in any way tampered with. That the Church consists of the laity as well as the clergy, and that each has its part to perform, were facts continually before the minds of its compilers in arranging the public offices. In the early years of the revival great stress was accordingly laid on the recitation of creeds and responses and the singing of psalms and hymns by the congregation, and the effect is very impressive at those churches where the services are still conducted on this principle. Impartial Romanists (*e.g.*, St. George Mivart) recognise this as one of the strong points of Anglicanism, and speak with admiration of the heartiness and enthusiasm of such services as compared with the Roman offices, in which the congregation can take little or no audible part. In spite, therefore, of the narrowness of the ultra-Gregorian school, their intentions were so far quite in accordance with the spirit of the Book of Common Prayer. We owe them a debt of gratitude for bringing out the rights of the congregation, and for providing for them according to their knowledge. The now almost universal practice of singing the Psalms and Canticles, instead of merely the *Gloria Patri* which concludes them, dates from the Gregorian revival, and is largely owing to the principles on which its advocates insisted. As I said before, we have got beyond them in their exclusive devotion to one species of music.

What we have to guard against now is that our services

do not become too musical. There is a disposition at many churches, not quite so advanced as those just mentioned as imitating the Roman use, to take the cathedral service as a model. As far as the congregation is concerned, the result is precisely the same, for where so much prominence is given to elaborate anthems and settings of the Canticles, to say nothing of difficult chants for the Psalms—frequently quite out of the reach of male voices in pitch—the share of the people is reduced to a wretched minimum.*

There is another very serious danger in the supremacy of music, and that is the degradation of preaching which seems likely to follow in consequence.

The old Puritan discourse of two hours† would be too oppressive. The miserable little composition, for which the word *sermonette* has been expressly coined, is scarcely more tolerable. The great masters of the revival did not err in this way. There has been a great falling off from the elaborate fulness of Dr. Pusey, from the classical elegance of Dr. Newman, among their successors, of many of whom it may be said in Bacon's words, 'They may have the same veins, but there is not the same blood in them as in those

---

* The contrast between the chaste and simple services of the Tractarians and those fashionable with some of their successors, musically and otherwise, might well be described in the words of Ernest Renan: 'Ma venue à Paris fut le passage d'une religion à une autre. Mon Christianisme de Bretagne ne ressemblait pas plus à celui que je trouvais ici qu'une vieille toile, dure comme une planche, ne ressemble à de la percale. Ce n'etait pas la même religion. Mes vieux prêtres, dans leur lourde chape romane, m'apparaissaient comme les mages, ayant les paroles de l'eternité ; maintenant, ce qu'on me présentait, c'etait une religion d'indienne et de calicot, une piété musquée, enrubanée, une devotion de petites bougies et de petits pots de fleurs, une théologie de demoiselles, sans solidité, d'un style indéfinissable, composite comme le frontispiece polychrome d'un livre d'Heures de chez Lebel.'—'Souvenirs.'

† There is a story of a preacher of this school who used to turn the hour-glass when half-way through his exhortation, with the significant remark, 'Brethren, let us have another glass before we part.'

of the ancients.' A favourite argument with those who cannot preach is that the sermon is not the principal object for which we come to church. This is perfectly true; but the sermon has its legitimate place in the church service, and the fact of a certain school having made too much of it is no reason for another disparaging it. The names of the great preachers of the revival ought to be enough to show that a good sermon is perfectly consistent with a proper regard for the Sacraments, and that it is at least as powerful an influence and attraction to certain minds as music.

In one sense the general falling off in preaching of late years may be regarded as an outcome of the revival, inasmuch as it is partly due to a reaction against the undue importance which the old evangelical school attached to preaching, and, further, because the extreme indolence of that school in the days preceding the revival—I mean as regards the ordinary work of a parish priest—has been succeeded by an almost restless activity. Where this activity is displayed in secular duties, as it too frequently is, which might be left to laymen, or left to take care of themselves, the remedy is of course in a clergyman's own hands.

Where the work done is entirely sacerdotal, one does not care to criticise. Yet here we are confronted with the curious fact that some of the most successful preachers in the highest sense, and judged by the results of their teaching, have been men otherwise most hardly pressed; such as, for instance, some of our bishops, who have had scarcely a moment to call their own, or men like Mr. Mackonochie and Mr. Lowder, whose lives have been spent from morning till night in parochial ministration, and that of a very trying kind to the intellect and bodily health.

Where the modern clergyman falls short of his Anglo-Catholic predecessors is chiefly in the neglect of *reading*. The Tractarians were essentially reading men. They were themselves well fed, or they would not have been able to feed others so well. The parochial clergy of to-day are, as a rule, so overloaded with external duties that their own education is apt to be neglected. And, in addition to not reading for their sermons, they have given up the practice of *writing* them.

In the early days of the revival the written sermon was the rule. A reaction has followed in favour of extemporaneous preaching, as it is called, and the result is that a flow of words about nothing is too often mistaken for eloquence, and that *thought* is conspicuously absent. Another distinguishing feature between the revivalists and their successors is that the former naturally made use of the sermon for the purpose of *teaching*. Now, sermons are too frequently mere exhortations, and the result is quite a surprising amount of ignorance, even in so-called Catholic congregations, about the *raison d'être* of Catholic doctrines, Church history, the history and structure of the Prayer-Book, and other matters, which the Tractarians taught well, and which might still be taught with advantage from the pulpit. For the fact is that although there never has been a time like the present for cheap books, people generally do not read in the proper sense of the word, and if they are to be taught systematically, it must be by others who have previously mastered the special subject. I have spoken freely in this matter because, in common with many laymen, I feel keenly the danger pointed out, and also that the remedies seem so simple.*

Perhaps the most obvious result of the revival is what has been called its 'Ritualistic development.' The extent to which this has spread could neither be foreseen nor provided for by the writers of the 'Tracts for the Times,' of whose doctrines it is of course the outcome. On the one hand it has involved the separation from the so-called Ritualists of many men of great ability who were ready to go with the

---

* It is by no means implied that the decline in preaching is confined to any special school. *All* schools have been more or less affected by the causes suggested.

movement in its purely intellectual and spiritual work; on the other hand, it cannot be denied that the most influential Tractarians, as far as they have lived to see the outward manifestation of their teaching, have consistently supported their successors in theory, whether they went with them in practice or not. For, in fact, nothing could be more natural or more logical than that the revival of the study of those ancient liturgies on which our Prayer-Book is based should be followed by a restoration of our services to the ancient models; that is, to the condition in which they were before the supremacy of Puritan and Calvinistic influences, and consequently by a restoration of those 'ornaments of the Church and of the ministers thereof' which were in use when the Prayer-Book was compiled, and which the Rubric tells us are still to be 'retained and be in use.' It is now generally admitted that in bringing this restoration about there has been a want of discretion, partly owing to a natural ignorance of what was good or bad ritual, of what was English or what was merely exotic, when the study of the subject had to be begun *ab initio*, and when there was no continuous practice to appeal to; partly out of an equally natural confusion between trifling details and matters of vital importance. On the part of the ritualists there has often been extravagance instead of decency and order. But the opposition to perfectly harmless and legitimate restorations has often been quite as absurd on the part of those who objected to them. It is remarkable, however, that, on the whole, there has been much less opposition to the elaborate ceremonial and ornate vestments more recently introduced than there was to the enunciation of the doctrines on which they are based, or to the very simple ritual which contented the Tractarians who preached and wrote those doctrines.

I have a very interesting work in the 'Farewell Letter to his Parishioners,' by the Rev. W. J. E. Bennett, of St. Paul's, Knightsbridge, and St. Barnabas, Pimlico, written on his resignation in 1851. Those who are not old enough to remember what happened may see from this little book that preaching in a surplice, the invocation before sermons, bowing at the Gloria and name of Jesus, the use of two candles on the altar, a movable altar cross, and altar flowers, besides such structural arrangements as a rood-screen, credence-table, aumbry, piscina, sedilia, etc., which are now thought nothing about, and are so general as to be no longer the marks of any particular school or party, were in their day the subjects of vehement discussion, some of them the occasion of public riots at the churches where they were introduced. The men who contended for these things have won the day, and have been succeeded by others who, beginning where they left off, have gone on to the full Eucharistic vestments and an amount of ceremony 'never dreamt of in the philosophy' of the Tractarians.

Although this development is one of the chief consequences of the Oxford Movement, there has been another influence at work to bring it about than a purely religious influence—I mean the revival of art in general, and of art in particular as an accessory to worship. Even this, however, is largely traceable to the stimulus of the Catholic Revival, or, if you prefer to put it so, to the general revival of which both were manifestations. This resuscitation of art in connection with religious worship was considered some years ago by Mr. Gladstone in an article on 'The Courses of Religious Thought,' written by him for the *Contemporary Review* at a time when prosecution was considered a proper remedy for ritualistic extravagance, and when the Public Worship Regulation Act was in embryo. I have not read the paper since its first appearance, but I think Mr. Gladstone's argument is that the restoration of coloured vestments and other ecclesiastical needlework, etc., was as natural a result of the modern art revival as the improved taste in crockery ware and wall-papers, and that Romish doctrine was no more involved in one than the other.

It was pointed out to me by a clerical friend at the time that Mr. Gladstone had merely looked at the subject from one point of view, namely, as answering to the requirements of an artistic worshipper, or of an artistic age, but had ignored its Divine aspect, viz., as a fitting investiture to the great act of Christian sacrifice. The latter was, of course, the reason why so much importance was attached to ancient costume and ceremonial by those who fought for their restoration; but it is quite possible that a merely æsthetic view was taken by the general public, who have gradually come to enjoy things which it would have been infinitely more difficult to restore in an inartistic age.

In Bacon's words, 'it is a light thing to be quoted in so serious a matter,' but there are people who think that the ecclesiastical revival has had a certain influence on the drama, and that the Church scenes in Shakespeare and Goethe, which have lately been produced with marvellous historical accuracy, would not have been possible before the Oxford Movement, when art was conspicuously absent in the actual worship of the English Church.

The whole question of ritual, as it has been reopened during the Catholic Revival, reminds one of the Eastern Iconoclastic Controversy of the eighth and ninth centuries. Then, as now, and probably always will be, the difference of opinion about externals is rooted in the essential differences in human nature. Where one person prefers simplicity, another prefers, perhaps even requires, such outward and visible aids to worship as are a positive hindrance to his neighbour. The Church seems now to recognise this fact, and its members have agreed to differ where there can never be a complete reconciliation. *In veste varietas sit, scissura non sit.*

Anyhow, no one can compare the Church of England services now with what they were in 1830 without acknowledging the influence of the Catholic Revival, even on the least Catholic of the schools of which the Church is composed.

Before I conclude, I should like to mention one or two external peculiarities adopted by the 'Puseyites,' as they were called, during the early stages of the movement. They had their origin in the ascetic character of the leading revivalists, and, being very generally adopted by their followers, becames badges of the party. Such was the custom of dressing in black, or, at least, of wearing a black neck-tie, which prevailed among gentlemen whose lives were as near an approach to the 'religious,' in the technical sense, as could be led by men outside a monastery.

The costume of the clergy was, of course, still more marked, and has gone through various modifications and developments according to the varying ideas of 'correctness' at different times, or as suggested by the inventive genius of ecclesiastical tailors. The particular form of waistcoat, for instance, which was known as the M.B. (= Mark of the Beast) was specially distinctive of the 'advanced' man; but as its use became more extended it lost its original significance, and was discontinued by the original wearer, and, in fact, became almost the badge of an Evangelical. Hats have gone through a similar process. The brims of felt hats have been gradually enlarged, till only men of strong opinions and great personal courage could venture out in them. A reaction has ensued, and the silk hat of the ordinary English gentleman, and of the Romish priest in this country, has become the usual covering of an 'advanced' head, the felt hat being left to the clergyman of mild Anglican views. Cassocks and neckties, too, have in their turn followed the various phases of the movement.

It became very general among the Anglo-Catholics to use the letter *S.* for Saint, instead of the *St.* of Protestants and Romanists. That custom also has become so general as to lose its party significance. The result is that the higher

Churchmen have now returned to the old form. The same remark applies to the practice of dating letters, etc., from the particular saint's day on which they were written, instead of the ordinary day of the month.

These harmless peculiarities have, to a great extent, disappeared as the revival has attained a more truly catholic and liberal character, and as Nature has asserted itself against the inevitable narrowness of a small and earnest party.

There were two matters of far greater importance on which the views of the advanced school had got to be too restricted to stand the test of time. Both had their origin in an ascetic view of life, right and proper enough probably at particular ages of the world, but which required considerable modification to suit the conditions of life in the nineteenth century. The first of these was the result of a reaction against the easy and self-indulgent habits characteristic of society and the Church before the Oxford Movement.

In the days when churches were closed from Sunday to Sunday it was not likely that the Ecclesiastical Calendar would be observed. Scarcely anybody kept the season of Lent, for instance, and there were still fewer who thought of keeping Friday. In fact, this day was found to be an extremely convenient one for dinner-parties, or going to the theatre. One of the first points, therefore, on which the revivalists insisted was the observance of fast-days as appointed by the Prayer-Book, and the necessity for a strict and disciplined life generally. Like all good things, however, this wholesome doctrine was pushed to excess by Anglo-Catholics of a later school, who seemed to take their idea of a proper physique from the attenuated figures in a stained-glass window. In this, however, it must be confessed that they carried out their doctrines most faithfully in their own persons, which they succeeded in reducing to the model of a St. Antony or Simeon Stylites, and which were only held together by continual courses of medicine and by the extreme energy of their minds. The Rev. T. Mozley, speaking of the time when he would not touch meat on a fast-day, tells us of the horror with which he had heard of a friend punishing himself on cold mutton simply because he disliked it ; and he adds that, at the time of writing, he had come to think him an extremely sensible man. This is an instance of the change of view that has occurred on the whole subject of self-discipline. As long as this is secured, people are less attentive to the letter of the law, and to the manner *how*.

The other point, which has also been modified by time, was an exaltation of celibacy, and a tendency consequently to look upon married people as somewhat lower in the scale of saintliness, and with lower prospects in the future state, than those who remained single. I do not know that this was ever formally stated in so many words, but I think I could lay my finger on passages in which the doctrine is suggested, and I know of clergymen who have implied as much in their sermons. In a case of this kind, however, where there was a continual argument to the contrary in human nature, the doctrine was not likely to become dangerous by its general acceptance. I am not aware now that it is ever heard ; and, as far as my personal experience goes, those who advocated it most violently have one after another joined the ranks of the Benedicts.

A fact that is sometimes urged against the Catholic revival is its 'Romeward tendency,' in proof of which its opponents quote, what there is no disputing and no need to dispute, that a certain number of people who were carried along with the current have been landed in the Roman Communion. As far as these secessions took place during the Oxford Movement, they were, as I have already shown, only partially traceable to the teaching of the movement party. There was then a 'wave of secession,' as it has been called ; and, looking at the state of the Church of England at the time, one cannot be surprised, however much one may regret it. But that movement and its consequences have so entirely altered the circumstances and character of the English Church that the temptations to leave her on the ground of finding something better elsewhere are now very rarely felt. Now and then one hears of a distinguished perversion—the Romanists take care that it shall be heard of—and, of course, there is a certain amount of proselytizing always going on at such places as the Brompton Oratory among people who may just as well belong to the Roman Church as any other. But the majority of English Churchmen, lay and clerical, are contented to remain where they are.

I mention this matter now to point out the effect on the Roman Church itself of the accession of such English gentlemen as Newman, Manning, F. W. Faber, F. Oakeley, and others who joined her about the same time and under similar motives. It is evident that the importation of such men has had the effect of introducing into the Roman Church here a powerful Anglican element which has had considerable influence as a corrective to the Italian and other foreign elements of which it must otherwise have chiefly consisted. With all their supposed Romish inclinations, these men had much more in common with the old hereditary Catholicism here, which was English first and Roman afterwards, than with the modern Ultramontanism introduced by the Italian mission on the establishment of the Roman hierarchy in 1850.

It is true that the Anglican converts have not always gone in the same direction within the Church of their adoption, but, on the whole, they have had sufficient weight and sufficient coherence among themselves to form the nucleus of a new school, combining the acceptance of the leading doctrines of Romanism with much of the modern scientific and philosophical spirit. There is, in fact, a strong resemblance between the school thus generated and the independent Gallican school across the water, both in simplicity of doctrine and ritual and in liberty of thought, in both of which points it presents an equally strong contrast to the tendencies of Ultramontanism. I may mention, in passing, that I am told those who wish to see the foreign and English parties at work side by side, and with an easy opportunity of contrasting them, may do so, or might have done so recently, at the Church of St. Etheldreda in Ely Place, where the simple services, as conducted by Father Lockhart, were very different to the 'religion musquée et enrubanée' of the Italian missioners in the same building. There are few Anglican churches more severely simple than Cardinal Newman's chapel at Edgbaston.

It is not to be wondered at, therefore, that this new school of English Romanism has gathered to itself much of the wealth and influence of the old Roman Catholic families, of the ducal houses who have never changed their religion, besides such modern intellect as has gone over since the establishment of the hierarchy. However satisfied the earlier seceders were in their own consciences with the step they had taken (and I suppose everyone else is convinced of their personal sincerity), there was necessarily much in their new religion to which they could never get accustomed. Partly, therefore, for themselves, partly perhaps with an eye to the progress of the Church of their adoption, partly unconsciously, and without any design at all, but simply by virtue of their irrepressible genius, they have done a good deal to Anglicize the Romish Church in this country. This Anglican character is observable in the preaching, the literature, the architecture, and the public worship of that Church; and if it is to make any progress here, it will be in proportion as it adheres to the principles thus infused into it.

If the English Church is true to its vocation, it need never fear the competition of its rival. But if in the course of time it should unhappily degenerate, say into its condition before the Oxford Movement, I am afraid there will still be a chance of the fulfilment of Macaulay's celebrated prophecy —viz., that the Romish religion will be supreme while the New Zealander sits on a broken arch of London Bridge sketching the ruins of St. Paul's. The possibility of such a result, remote though it be, lies in the Anglican character given to the Romish Church by those who have joined her from the Church of their baptism. Men knowing the strength and weakness of the English Church, men acquainted with every point of the controversy between England and Rome, men educated at English Universities, men fully equipped in literature and philosophy, men who can preach and write, men well read in theology, and, what is more, in English life and character, have thought it right to transfer their allegiance to the Roman camp, and have furnished it with the weapons which can alone make it formidable in this country.

It will be a bad day for the English Church if it is ever tempted to rely on the privileges supposed to be conferred by Establishment instead of those Catholic principles which are its surest foundation.

THE END.

www.ingramcontent.com/pod-product-compliance
Lightning Source LLC
Chambersburg PA
CBHW030247170426
43202CB00009B/657